D1029605

WITHDRAWN

A Sacred Duty

A Sacred Duty

Ester Rasband
with
Richard Wilkins

Bookcraft
Salt Lake City, Utah

To Jim and to Melany, whose entry into our lives has been life-giving, life-nurturing, and life-sustaining.

Ester and Richard

Library of Congress Catalog Card Number 99-95579
ISBN 1-57008-687-7

First Printing, 1999

Printed in the United States of America

CONTENTS

ACKNOWLEDGMENTS

We are indebted to Cory Maxwell at Bookcraft who originally conceived of a book about Richard's amazing Istanbul experience. We also thank Susan Roylance, who not only was largely responsible for Richard's involvement in the Istanbul Conference but was later generous with materials as well as interview time to help Ester understand the materials' import. We thank all those (too many to list) who wrote the volumes of information and recorded impressions that added to that understanding.

We also wish to thank George Bickerstaff, Jana Erickson, and the others at Bookcraft who contributed to the project, and our families who gave both encouragement and criticism throughout the creative process.

Richard would like to express his particular thanks to Brigham Young University President Merrill J. Bateman and Dean Reese Hansen of the J. Reuben Clark Law School for their support of NGO Family Voice: The World Family Policy Center. Kathryn Balmforth, Cory Leonard, and Terrance Olson also have enthusiastically given of their time and effort to continue the work begun in Istanbul.

Finally, we are grateful to each other for what has been a delightful and rewarding collaboration.

Note on the Format

In this book Ester Rasband tells Richard Wilkins's story as he related it to her. At times, however, Richard's first-person reflections on his experiences are added. To distinguish between authors, text in Richard's voice will be **set in this type** and will be separated from Ester's narration by a star ✸.

CHAPTER 1

The Proclamation

It was September 1995. Bishop Richard Wilkins, nothing if not dutiful, attended the women's satellite broadcast. He had been invited to do so, and he went. Not that it was an unpleasant assignment. It was certainly agreeable to sit next to his wife, Melany, in church. That didn't often happen, and he liked it.

Sister Jack spoke; then Sister Okazaki and Sister Clyde. He was struck, as he had been before, with how articulate they were. The meeting was going well.

His mind wandered for a moment to other things. He looked at his wife and, almost audibly in his head, thought of the love and admiration he felt for her. Her indispensable support was part of everything he did. Her intellect; her spirit. What an energy source she was to him! Sometimes he thought about people who were to one degree or another alone, who didn't have the unity he felt with Melany. It made him sad.

As the bishop looked around the room, he saw some of the women from his ward. He reflected that there was so much strength in them, so much faith. He knew of their goodness as only a bishop could. He depended on them and they were there as needed. He was humbly grateful.

The prophet went to the pulpit and Richard snapped to attention. The collective respect was profound. President Hinckley told the congregation his talk might go long. He said it with humor, and the resultant laughter was relaxing. When he looked into their eyes one felt that he saw the joys and concerns of each age group, each individual. That he honored womanhood was clear, and the tenderness of his feelings toward them couldn't help but pierce their hearts. He talked about their blessings and their challenges. He read a letter from a single mother who, with the Lord's help, had raised a righteous family. He mentioned briefly those who were burdened with "an affinity for the same sex," and his love and sympathy reached out to all.

Momentarily he was silent. Then: "With so much of sophistry that is passed off as truth, with so much of deception concerning standards and values, with so much of allurement and enticement to take on the slow stain of the world, we have felt to warn and forewarn. In furtherance of this we of the First Presidency and the Council of the Twelve Apostles now issue a Proclamation to the Church, and to the world, as a declaration and reaffirmation of standards, doctrines, and practices relative to the family which the prophets, seers, and revelators of this church have repeatedly stated throughout its history. I now take the opportunity of reading to you this proclamation."

And he did just that. *The Family, A Proclamation to the World.* His tone was serious. Momentous, even.

In closing he was yet more tender than before: "May the Lord bless you my beloved sisters; you are the guardians of the hearth. . . . No other work reaches so close to divinity as does the nurturing of the sons and daughters of God. . . . May you be endowed with wisdom beyond your own."

Richard could not but be touched by the spirit of utter kindness President Hinckley radiated. He thought the prophet a man who reached beyond the world entirely. It was comforting to be so led. It was an escape from the world just to be in his presence. The Proclamation, however—well, in a smiling, nodding way—he thought that it was "nice" and he realized he was damning it with faint praise. *Useful* would not be the word he would have chosen. Powerful? Certainly not. He had come to feel that all righteous sources were powerless where issues such as these were concerned.

I'm a constitutional lawyer—a law professor. In this capacity I was always a lawyer-activist on what I considered legal and moral issues. I'd been doing abortion law—abortion policy—since I graduated from law school in 1979. In 1982, as an assistant solicitor general in the Reagan administration, I wrote the brief that Rex Lee argued before the Supreme Court, for *Akron Center for Reproductive Health v. The State of Ohio*. It was an effort to overturn *Roe v. Wade,* an effort which of course failed. Both Rex and I were maligned in the *New York Times,* not to mention publications of lesser reputation. It was my first experience with public vilification. I hated how it made me feel.

Although the *Akron* case had not succeeded in its ultimate objective, still there seemed to be some softening in the Court regarding *Roe,* and many of us were hopeful that eventually it could be overturned. By the end of a decade, however, the Court had instead hardened their position. Whereas in 1982 we had lost a battle, by 1992 we had lost the war.

When the state of Utah began to fight what I later came to call the "Utah Abortion Wars" it remained only to regulate abortion to the maximum extent we could while still complying with the Supreme Court rulings. I drafted legislation. Dedicated pro-abortionists, however, wanted no regulation at all.

For four long years we fought the battle in the legislature, in the courts, and, unfortunately, in the media. I am not combative by nature and I did not thrive on constant contact with angry, determined people who wanted to discredit and even eradicate me. The anger came from both sides of the debate. As I strove for a workable solution, I satisfied no one.

It was, in fact, a pro-life extremist who called my home one day, just as my children were coming home from school at three o'clock in the afternoon, to tell me that someone had been "dispatched" to kill me. For weeks afterward my family lived with fear while police protection hovered over us.

By the time I attended that broadcast in 1995 I considered the "Utah Abortion Wars" over, but the clamor on the national scene over our (albeit limited) successes was still deafening.

Richard's real cynicism in these matters was interrupted only by periods of more overt anger. He considered both to be his experiential right. Little by little he had developed a kind of hardness, and there was an edge to everything he was doing. He sought sweet escape from it in Melany and the children—and sometimes his ward. But even that didn't always work, and there was less and less time with his family anyway. He felt indignant about that too.

His involvement in legal and social issues was a good thing. He knew it was. He wanted to do what was right, and the Spirit had not spared in giving him a witness that reassured him. Still, even a good thing can leave some hurt in its shadow when the victories are not forthcoming and the criticism is intense. Gradually the sense of sacrifice gives way to a sentiment of deprivation and resentment. Richard's personal life was suffering. He was tight as a fist all the time. Melany felt it. His children felt it.

I'd reached a point where, although I hadn't put it into words, I think I actually believed my job was to be the bitter cynic—to sit back and write law review articles saying how degraded and "down the tubes" our society had become. I was just going to wag my finger at everybody and be hard and nasty and clench my fist and grind my teeth. It was not a positive thing for my family, and it was not a happy thing for me.

On the way home Melany mentioned the Proclamation, and Richard voiced aloud his original thought: "It's nice," he said.

It was a few days later when a copy of the Proclamation came across the desk of Professor Wilkins at the law school. Richard experienced an unexpected simple witness that this was the doctrine of the Church, but it was so fleeting and so unexplained that he all but ignored it.

If I did think anything about it, I had this kind of cynical feeling: This is just going to do nothing, because the world is so far beyond any of the stuff that this talks about. They might as well just hang this up!

At no point did Richard guess, during those next six months, that the Proclamation on the Family would become his balm of Gilead, the "oil to make his face to shine, and [the] bread which strengtheneth man's heart" (Psalm 104:15).

CHAPTER 2

Romance Denied

The late winter and spring of 1996 was shaping up to be a wild ride for the Wilkins family. In addition to his responsibilities at the law school, Richard was always in great demand as a consultant in constitutional law. It was this consulting, in fact, that created the larger part of the family's income.

It pleased Richard to be such a good provider. He never had a *love* of money. His heart was too full of commitment—too full of inclination to his family and his duty (though, seemingly, not always in that order) for there to be enough room left for the *love* of money. But the *comfort* of it was enjoyable. And it felt good that his children wanted for nothing. Adding his obligations as a bishop to his crowded professional life, Richard's world was always full, always bustling.

Nevertheless, this particular spring he intended to add even more to his plate. He and Melany had their eyes on a beautiful building site high up on Provo's bench, and they had decided it was time to build their dream house. Brooke, their daughter and the oldest of their four children, was almost twenty. Brinton would soon graduate from high school, and Claire had already entered it. Only Rex, their four-year-old, was young enough to always remember the house they would build as his real homestead. If it was ever to be home to all of them, the building process had to begin.

Something else, though, was also in the works; something that Richard had planned for a long time. He couldn't remember when the idea had first occurred to him; probably years ago—maybe even twenty-five years ago—and the time had finally come.

Richard and Melany met in a Sunday School class when they were both fifteen years old. By the time they starred opposite one another in their high school production of *Fiddler on the Roof* three years later, Richard was irreversibly smitten. Their permanent union created a theater family—much the same way that some have football or baseball families. The theater was the way they taught their children to honor the team effort, to experience the discipline of showing up when they didn't want to do it, and to meet high demands of memorization and following direction. Playing a character required them to see another's point of view and to enter into it with empathy. The stage was their education, their entertainment, and their exercise. It was also often their avenue of expression.

It had been twenty-five years since Melany and I first played Golde and Tevye and faced one another on the stage of Brighton High School to sing that beautiful love song at the end of "Fiddler." After all the years of encountering the unforeseen together, we could now sing that song with more significance than we had in 1971.

Tevye: Then you love me?
Golde: I suppose I do.
Tevye: And I suppose I love you, too.
Both: It doesn't change a thing, but even so, after twenty-five years, it's nice to know.

It was not difficult to convince our friends at the Hale Theater that this was the year they should produce *Fiddler on the Roof.* Melany and I were Tevye and Golde again in this anniversary year, and it was made even more meaningful because all of our children were either in the cast or involved in the management. June 10 was scheduled to be the closing night. I planned a surprise party for Melany after that final performance. I invited friends who would make it memorable, and I ordered twenty-five red roses—to be delivered to my wife.

At some level Richard probably knew that the party was even more for him than it was for his wife. He needed the celebration of romance, the reminder of the gentleness in his life.

And so it was that, amidst the happy squeezing-in of house plans and rehearsals, amidst a household filled with shouts of "Tradition!" and the sweetness of "Sunrise, Sunset," the Wilkins family prepared—or rather was totally *un*prepared—for the change that would come into their life that summer.

It was most likely February (Richard remembers now only that it was still winter) when Susan Roylance called Richard at his office. Susan was, at that time, president of United Families International. She was also his good friend from the days of the "Utah Abortion Wars." Ever since those days Susan had been in contact with Richard, soliciting his input in one way or another. She was as patient and tireless with him as she was with the rest of her efforts in defense of causes that promoted the family.

Several months earlier, while I was trying a case before the Utah Supreme Court, I happened to look out at the gallery and saw Susan there. I reasoned that she probably needed to see me for something, but the session was a long one and I was frankly surprised that she endured it for the three hours it took before I had a break. Even then I could give her only about five minutes.

She had just returned from a PrepCom[1] in New York following up on the Beijing Women's Conference, which had been held in 1995. She was concerned. "In New York, they talked about the things they were writing as if they would really make a difference—I mean, you know, as if they'd be enforceable. Are they? Do the policy recommendations of the United Nations make any real difference?"

My response was quick and necessarily brief: "I don't think so, Susan, no. But I'll look into it for you."

"Good. Thank you," Susan said. "And Richard, could you write a couple of pages for me about your findings. I'm putting a book together about the traditional family in peril, and I'd like to include what you find."

Richard acquiesced, and he produced what turned out to be a short chapter in her book. How could he say no to someone who gave as much as Susan gave? He simply had to do it. Besides, he was quite surprised by what he found in his limited research. "Ill-conceived or otherwise unsound international declarations pose dangers," he wrote, "not because they directly displace existing American law, but because they inevitably shape that law." Richard was not an international lawyer, and Susan's request had prompted his first foray into its research. It had fleetingly piqued his interest. But that had been months ago.

When Susan telephoned Richard at his office that fateful wintry day in 1996, the book that included Richard's short piece on United Nations influence had already been published. She had another request: "Richard," she said, "there's a Habitat II Conference in Istanbul in early June. I think you ought to go." Richard was familiar with Habitat II. It was to be a United Nations conference to establish an agenda: a sort of statement of intent to influence world communities. He was peripherally aware that it would probably be used as a condition of aid—perhaps aid from private sources. But if he were to go, he didn't see any way at all that he could be anything but a whipping boy. He quickly responded that June was impossible and that, anyway, he didn't see why he should.

"You should go and do something."

"What?"

"I don't know. Something. There will be 25,000 participants at the conference, and the outcome of the deliberations will be a document that, if your paper was right, could provide an international legal climate for the far-reaching future.

"Very few will be there who hold traditional family values, Richard. The Cairo Conference on Population and the Beijing Conference on Women—all the things they have in their documents will be right up front to be included in this agenda. They aren't good for the family, Richard. You need to go and do something."

Nevertheless, Richard answered that he was sorry. The timing was wrong. And besides, he honestly hadn't the hope to fight the battle.

I had no reason to believe that we could make a difference. Susan said "do something," but she didn't know what. I certainly didn't know what. Nothing I had done before had ever changed the world. I knew the other side had a well-oiled machine. I had felt its wrath already. My plans were for an early summer of beauty and romance—a family time that I had envisioned for years. I wasn't going to sacrifice it.

I told Melany about Susan's request. From the beginning she felt I ought to go, but the idea of giving up my dream for days of fruitless persecution was not appealing to me. I prayed about it, of course, but my prayers were more in the nature of "Please, I don't want to go" than they were "I'll go where you want me to go." I suppose I was fiddling on the roof. Like Tevye, I was "trying to scratch out a pleasant simple tune without breaking [my] neck."[2] It wasn't going to work.

I started waking up in the night thinking about Istanbul. It was a nagging consciousness that wouldn't go away. Susan kept calling—sensing, I suppose, a weakening of my resolve. And Melany was quietly constant in her belief that it was right. Eventually "no" changed to "maybe." I inquired about budget for it at the law school. There was none. There were other bits of information I wanted before I made the decision. Every answer justified my inclination to refuse. But there were still those sleepless nights. Unpleasant as I knew it was bound to be, it was my duty. Finally, "maybe" changed to "yes." Working with Bradley Roylance, a law student, I hastily put together a paper. It seemed I should at least submit something for the NGO (Non-Governmental Organization) seminars. I knew that hundreds of papers were submitted. But I didn't want to go empty-handed.

As for the play, fortunately it had been double-cast. The schedule was changed so that the other Tevye, my lifelong friend Merrill Dodge, would be in my place on June 10. Merrill had at one time dated Melany, and I felt as though now he would be my proxy. It was melancholy, I know, but I admit it occurred to me. I put it out of my mind.

✡

The date for the Istanbul Conference approached, and circumstances did not come together to make it easier for Richard. As it happened, by the time he was ready to leave there was a "sold" sign on their home. He felt that once again he was leaving Melany with the burden of it all.

Richard looked in the mirror the day before he left. He supposed that he ought to shave off the beard; but he wasn't entirely ready to give up being Tevye. Besides, if he did he was afraid that his tan line would make him look like a raccoon. He trimmed the beard instead and told himself that he would shave when he got home from Istanbul. He packed his suitcase. He sighed. He was already travel-weary in his heart. When he was ready to close the case, Melany came into the room. She had a piece of paper in her hand. She slipped it in on top of his clothes. "You may need this," she said. It was the Proclamation on the Family.

CHAPTER 3

Bearded and Tweedy

Richard boarded his plane in Salt Lake City on Sunday afternoon and changed planes late that night in New York. The layover was welcome. His lengthy six-foot-two frame did not quite fit into economy class seating, and stretching his legs at JFK felt so good that it even cleared his head a bit. He was not hungry and he didn't feel like reading. He just walked—and stayed close to the boarding area.

By the time Richard was finally in the air Istanbul-bound, it was already well past the time when he would have been in bed. But he was wide awake. He watched the New York skyline until it was gone, then stared out at the blackness. It was only a brief period before the darkness began to dissipate. He was flying into the sunrise. Richard could hardly take his eyes off the strange sensation of time-lapsed photography. Still, it didn't quite distract him from worrying over what his mission might entail. He was apprehensive. The phenomenon of the sunrise was not the only thing keeping him from sleep.

I am not an international lawyer. I'm accustomed to working in a field where I am established as an expert. My publications are usually the result of months—even years—of exacting thoroughness. Law professors are anything but willing to go out on a limb when their entire learning and education on something is about four weeks old. Yet here I was, sitting on an airplane that had in its belly a suitcase containing three hundred copies of a paper that had been written in a matter of days regarding an area about which I knew little when measured by my own professional standard. I hadn't put in the years of study that usually made me intellectually confident. I kept coming back to wondering why I was going at all. "Do something," Susan had said, and I was on my way to Turkey. It was bizarre.

I suppose it should have been some reassurance to me that I believed few would hear the little workshop I had been nominated to present. The odds were small indeed that anyone would want a copy of my paper. At that thought, I began to feel ridiculous that I had brought so many copies. Nothing was reassuring. Here I was, on an airplane to Istanbul, hurtling into the sun and out of my comfort zone. "Apprehensive" is probably too light a word to describe what was for me a very heavy feeling.

The plane landed in Istanbul and Richard summoned all his courage to enter a new world "not knowing beforehand the things which [he] should do" (see 1 Nephi 4:6).

Susan Roylance met Richard's airplane and deftly managed the retrieval of his luggage and his movement through the maze that was Istanbul's international airport. "It's important that you get accredited right away," Susan said. "We'll go directly to the NGO Forum and get that done."

✳

A UN conference operates as an international joint venture between participating governments and the worldwide private sector. The official delegates, who come to a UN conference representing their governments, conduct the negotiating and drafting sessions. They wear green badges. While the sessions for official delegates are proceeding, and in separate facilities, representatives from private-sector UN-accredited "Non-Governmental Organizations" (NGOs) conduct an NGO Forum at which they present lectures, workshops, and informational materials related to the conference. The hope is that all these activities will persuade the official delegates to favor the NGO point of view in official declarations. The NGO representatives wear red badges, which quite literally mean "stop" as far as some of the meetings are concerned. The activities at the NGO Forum attract an occasional television or newspaper reporter, and the NGO representatives spend a good deal of time in lobbying and/or supporting the delegates.

The NGO Forum, of course, is also somewhat exclusive. The only people who are allowed full participation in that forum are representatives of recognized Non-Governmental Organizations and established international groups. I was a professor at the BYU Law School, and since a law school does not fit either of those descriptions I went to the conference sponsored by the university's David M. Kennedy Center for International Studies. When the United Nations clerks filled out the necessary forms to allow me to register, the limited space allowed for only a kind of shorthand; so "David M." was dropped from the name. I had hardly noticed it. It seemed like an appropriate abbreviation.

✳

The building assigned to the NGO Forum had clearly merited pride at one time. Its neoclassic facade was not now beautiful, but its crumbling Corinthian pillars cried out as with a bygone glory. Susan and Richard entered together and approached the woman at the desk. When it was Richard's turn the woman asked, "You're from the Kennedy Center?" Richard answered that yes, he was.

The woman at the desk treated Richard with a respect he hadn't expected. Susan had told him that academics were treated with more deference than the others, and in fact that seemed to be what was happening. It crossed his mind that it was inappropriate for him to be getting such regard when he stood there with someone like Susan, whose untiring, selfless service ought to give her more consideration than should be given to his academic status.

The woman excused herself, then went to the other end of the table and chatted with someone who looked over her glasses at Richard and smiled. On returning, the first woman asked Richard if he had come prepared to present anything. Actually, he said, he had brought three hundred copies of a paper he had prepared for that purpose. She was clearly pleased. She asked for a copy of the paper; and since Richard was standing there with all of his luggage, he told her he had it right at hand.

Right at hand may have been a little optimistic. The copies occupied a very old hard-sided Samsonite suitcase. It was red in color and awkward in hardware. Richard had trouble getting it open, and when he finally succeeded it gave way with a springing action that threw the copies in every direction. He quickly rescued one and gave it to the woman. She looked at it briefly. "Oh, this looks very interesting. Can you stay here for a second?"

She scurried off again without explanation. Richard was glad for the moment in which to gather the far-flung copies back into his scuffed-up old suitcase. When the woman came back a second time, she repeated: "This looks very interesting. Now, you're a law professor, is that correct?" Richard answered that yes, he was a law professor.

"You're a law professor from the Kennedy Center?" Again he answered yes. (All of that was on the papers he had given her, but he guessed that the accreditation people always confirmed such things.)

"Would you be interested in presenting this paper?"

Richard answered that he surely would.

"We're inviting certain scholars to make formal presentations, and we have an opening tomorrow evening. We'd like to hear from you then. It's the second night of the conference. Can you be ready that soon?"

Richard replied, "Certainly." She signed him up; took his picture; and accredited him as Professor Richard G. Wilkins from the Kennedy Center for International Studies.

It didn't surprise Susan Roylance that Richard had been scheduled into a large room. She had in fact requested that his workshop be given a large room and translation services. The distinction between formal and informal was not something either of them gave any thought to.

Richard was eager to get to the hotel, but Susan had another stop in mind. They went to a hotel room where members of the Caucus for Stable Communities were struggling to find just the right language for some amendments they wanted to present to be considered for inclusion in the Habitat Agenda. Richard said his "how-do-you-dos" and sat down to read the materials he was given. He was by now exhausted. His mind was working only by rote. But in spite of his fatigue, his legal expertise was too much a part of him to be seriously impaired. He read the group's documents and found them to be, in some cases, filled with language that would accomplish the exact opposite of their intent. He stayed for a short while to listen to the group's deliberations and then asked that he be excused to check in at his hotel. They thanked him. They were obviously pleased to have been rescued from their potential errors.

Richard went, finally, to the Ulubat Hotel. It was disquieting to see bunkers of machine gun nests surrounding the place—sandbags and barbed wire everywhere—but for some merciful reason it did not even occur to Richard to fear imprisonment or hostage taking. They registered. The cost was $6 per night.

The Ulubat was a well-worn little place euphemistically labeled "tourist class." The whole of the establishment was in desperate need of paint and higher-wattage lightbulbs. Shabby as it was, though, it was clean—well, clean *enough* in such dim light. He wouldn't be sharing his bed with vermin.

Both the rooms and the bathroom facilities were shared with other lodgers and were not exactly of a type that a western guest might find familiar. On the floor of the rooms were plywood platforms obviously intended to be beds. They were about thirty inches wide and less than six feet long. For a mattress each had a piece of cotton ticking covered by a sheet, and they got a clean sheet once a week. Breakfast was included. The menu was bread and hot water. For the other guests they offered instant coffee or tea to put in it. For Richard and his thirty-six United Families comrades, it was bread and hot water.

Richard's roommate was Bradley Stone, the chairman of a financial network in Salt Lake City and a stalwart in United Families. Brad and the others from United Families had already registered at the Ulubat when Richard arrived. At least he would be able to associate the stay with good company. Alone it might have been too depressing to bear.

Richard unpacked a few things and took an encompassing glance around the room. "Six dollars," he thought, "and worth every penny of it."

Now registered and initiated (or so he thought) into the business of the conference, Richard was all at once possessed of a new energy. He began to give way to the excitement of being in such an exotic part of the world. He had not traveled outside the United States since his mission to Italy some twenty or so years earlier, and now here he was in *Istanbul!* Istanbul, the city built on two continents and spanning seven hills—a city said to unite cultures as well as continents. Anticipation crowded everything else from Richard's mind. He quickly stowed his luggage and left the hotel with a few of the United Families contingent, forgetting completely that he had not slept in more than twenty-four hours. He bought a map at a nearby stand.

What I wanted most to see was the Suleymaniye Mosque. *National Geographic* had done a piece on Suleyman the Great just the past summer, and it had piqued my interest. I opened the large map and searched to find my objective. The map, however, notwithstanding its large size, was woefully incomplete. Narrow little streets were not marked on it, and larger ones often were misplaced. I couldn't see a marking for the Suleymaniye Mosque at all. Some of the women from United Families wanted to see the Sultan Ahmet Mosque (better known as the Blue Mosque), and that, being the more common tourist site, was clearly marked and easy to find. We headed there.

After marveling at the blue-stenciled interior of the Sultan Ahmet Mosque, it was a short walk for them across a pedestrian mall to the Hagia Sophia, a magnificent domed basilica built almost fifteen hundred years ago. The structure and its history were impressive. It was built in the Constantinople of Justinian the First. As Richard was leaving, however, his eye was drawn even more intently to a small rug shop in the corner of the wall surrounding the mosque.

The proprietor of the rug shop was obviously there for western tourists. He was even dressed in blue jeans with an enormous silver belt buckle.

I stopped to look at the stack of rugs. After all, I had spent the spring poring over plans for a house that we would soon build—a house with what seemed like acres of hardwood floors. We would need rugs. I thought it a lovely idea for souvenirs of the trip.

The salesman was skillful at gaining Richard's trust—as well as at recognizing a customer who would offer little resistance. He made the bargains sound impossible to refuse. The women from United Families helped with the selection process—a great service, inasmuch as Richard is color blind—and within a couple of hours Richard proffered his Master-Card and left the little shop in the corner of the Hagia Sophia with two large and (the ladies assured him) beautiful rugs. Richard knew nothing of such things, but the salesman "guaranteed" him that the number of knots in the handtied beauties made them of extraordinary quality. They would be perfect for the house on the hill.

Amazed at the amount of time that had passed, and now suddenly remembering their need for rest, Richard and the others headed back to the Ulubat and settled down for the night on their plywood beds. Richard's feet hung over the edge no matter how he tried to adjust himself, but it bothered him for only a few minutes because he soon fell soundly asleep.

The next morning when we arrived at the NGO Forum, one of the first things that caught my eye was a yellow flyer pinned to a bulletin board announcing my speech that evening in a large central room. It declared that translation services were being provided by the United Nations interpreters, and it treated the whole event as if it were to be quite extraordinary. I read it again and there was no question that the speaker was I: "Professor Richard Wilkins of the Kennedy Center." They were even correct on the title of my speech: "The Impact of UN Conference Declarations on International and Domestic Law." All of a sudden I was even more afraid than I had been before.

The evening meetings—the "formal" meetings—it seems were different from the other workshops. The woman at the accreditation desk must have thought I knew that.

All that day Richard and his friends from the Ulubat saw yellow flyers everywhere. They were posted and distributed in every corner of the NGO Forum. And Richard was surprised beyond measure when he discovered that the flyers were also being distributed up on the hill at the posh Hilton Hotel—the place where the green-badged delegates themselves were holding the meetings that would form the recommendations for the final Habitat II agenda. No matter where he looked, Richard saw the yellow flyer with his name on it, and with the name of the paper of which he was not altogether professionally proud.

When evening came and Richard walked with trepidation into the largest auditorium in the NGO Forum, he looked out and saw every seat filled and many people standing. A few were NGO representatives that he recognized from the booths or from chance meetings during the day. Many, however, were wearing those green badges. The flyers up at the Hilton had apparently borne fruit.

It's probably just as well that I didn't know at the time that the meeting was attended by the chief justice of the Supreme Court of Pakistan, by the chief justice from India, by two members of the British House of Lords, and by the ambassadors from Saudi Arabia and the United Arab Emirates. There were also official people from Australia and Canada. It was intimidating enough just knowing that I was about to give a paper concerning which, at that time, I was still uncertain. I felt like a law student doing a moot court.

Nevertheless, when I got up to speak I had the rapt attention of the audience.

Richard swallowed hard and began to read:

"The United Nations General Assembly periodically convenes world conferences on issues of global concern. . . ."

It was necessary to give the group something of the history of international law. Richard began at the 1658 Treaty of Westphalia and traced the evolution of international law from agreements that governed only the relations of nation states to modern agreements with their increasing focus on the behavior of individuals within those nation states.

Richard's training in the theater enabled him to know when he had an audience's concentration. He had it and he knew it. His voice became a little stronger, a little bolder. He plunged into the body of his paper.

"This article explores the impact of UN conferences not only upon international law but also upon the domestic law of conference participants. . . ."

Richard explained the difference between customary law and formal treaty law. It was all very technical as he talked about the morass of customs and treaties and, as it turned out, United Nations declarations. Richard was aware that the delegates were not necessarily able to grasp every nuance of international law. He worried for only a moment that he might lose them. But they were still rapt. He continued.

He talked most of all about how UN declarations, even though usually considered nonbinding, can ever more quickly be construed as "customary" international law.

He cited one case from a United States court that was decided on the basis of a UN document which had not been ratified by the U.S. Senate. As far as the United States was concerned, however, the single case, with its limited influence, seemed of less portent than the shaping of regulations under the influence of the conference declarations.

"In the United States, for example," Richard pointed out, "the Clinton Administration has formed an inter-agency task force and commission to implement the Beijing document. The task force and commission educate various federal agencies regarding Beijing recommendations and implement the document through domestic regulations. As a result, portions of the Beijing document have been incorporated directly into United States policy—without formal adoption of that document (or its stated objectives) by the United States legislature."

Richard called their attention to other countries as well that were citing unratified UN documents as customary international law. Richard had several examples. When he looked down into the eyes of his audience, his confidence was no longer lacking.

". . . Each conference builds upon language used and objectives sought in preceding conferences and, as a result, forms an important link in a chain that inevitably encircles the international community. . . . Perhaps most important, however, conference documents—although not formally binding upon participating states—over time develop the force of customary international law and serve as important resources in the interpretation (and sometimes development) of the domestic policy of participating nations.

"This final point suggests that all participating nations should take very seriously indeed the language they incorporate into a UN declaration. . . . That same language . . . may well become binding tomorrow."[3]

When Richard concluded, his nervousness revisited him. It needn't have. Within moments he was thronged by people asking for copies of his remarks. "I didn't think what we did here made any real difference," one official was saying. "This is frightening to contemplate!" came from another man wearing an official badge. The chief justice from India was frank: "I don't believe you. My nation doesn't really intend to enforce any of this. We negotiate and sign these agreements because we want to go home. And we intend to ignore them."

From every side came requests for copies, and Richard fumbled to open the red suitcase again. As delegates stopped to ask questions, he heard cries of "copies" over the din, and he made a halting sort of motion toward the case as he nodded his head in what seemed like several directions at once. Even Melinda Kimball, the head of the United States delegation, said that she hadn't been aware of the influences he outlined and she asked for multiple copies to take back to her delegation. In a matter of minutes people realized that the case was empty and asked where they could get more copies. Richard was overwhelmed. "Leave your name and where we can reach you. We'll see that you get copies," he promised, not even thinking it through.

In the middle of that moment, with people clamoring for copies and avowing surprise, Richard was seized with a certain skepticism. He was unsure whether this was a new concept to the delegates or simply one that they had chosen to ignore. Perhaps he had only forced them to look at something that was uncomfortable, something that, if they fully faced it, might interfere with their ability to go along and get along. Perhaps his duty, after all, was not to educate so much as it was to strengthen. And strength, he soon found, was going to be needed.

The fact is that these international conferences mean something. They mean something because they create customary norms. Customary international law requires two things: first, it requires some sort of recognition by nations that this is the rule; and second, it requires indication of their intent to be bound by that rule. Now, when nations get together and they negotiate these documents—a document such as the Habitat Agenda was going to be—they do both of these things: they recognize that this is the rule and then they sign this document saying, "We intend to act on these principles." In other words, they evidence their intent to be bound.

What my paper said was: "Slow down and look at this. You're creating binding law by a process that doesn't have good democratic input. The people back home don't know the rules you're coming up with. And furthermore, it appears that the people back home would disagree with a lot of these rules."

On that Tuesday night—the day after I arrived—I had not yet fully appreciated the accuracy and extent of what I was saying. Although I had heard things from people that led me to believe there was inadequate input in these documents, I soon came to understand that the documents produced were almost wholly influenced by special interest groups.

As the crowd around Richard dwindled, he was approached by some women who were far from captivated by his paper. They were, in fact, hostile in the extreme. He had certainly not expected the intensely positive response that his paper seemed to generate, but the negative reaction included a charge that was at least as much of a surprise:

"How dare you misrepresent yourself in order to present such nonsense?" (The language has been cleaned up considerably for this publication.)

"Misrepresent?" Richard was genuinely confused.

"Yes, misrepresent! *You're* not from Harvard!"

"Well, I never pretended to be." Richard was still blank.

"Kennedy Center! Ha! You jerk!" (Language laundered again.)

The accusation startled him. Then suddenly, he saw the error. The woman at the accreditation desk, the flyers, the UN translators—everything instantly made sense.

"I'm from the David M. Kennedy Center for International Relations, not the John F. Kennedy School of Government. The UN clerks shortened it to 'The Kennedy Center.' It's an acceptable shorthand. We use it. Had I known that there was a mistaken identity I most certainly would have corrected it."

The women sneered at his "excuse." Although their agenda had not been mentioned, in a fundamental way it had been exposed, and they were angry. As they moved away, Richard caught a glimpse of himself in a stained old mirror on a nearby wall. For the first time he could understand their ire. He took an objective look. There he stood, bearded and tweedy, looking for all the world like the Eastern U.S. Intellectual Establishment. The only thing that would have made the picture more stereotypical might have been a pipe in his pocket. He was a far cry from the clean-cut BYU type of professor. But he had had no dishonest intent, and the ringing reaction to his paper made it clear to Richard that it was sorely needed.

By the time he went back to the Ulubat that night he was almost amused that his bearded and tweedy appearance might have been what afforded him this incredible opportunity. When he offered his prayers, he thanked his Heavenly Father for the amazing mistaken identity.

CHAPTER 4

We the People

For the next few days Richard spent his daylight hours up
on the hill at the Hilton Hotel lobbying the official delegates of
the conference. He found it less difficult than he would have
thought. Doors had been opened by his presentation.

The Habitat II Conference was intended to build on the accomplishments of several other United Nations conferences,
but on two previous conferences in particular: The 1994 Cairo
Conference on Population and Development, and the 1995
Beijing World Conference on Women.

The declaration that came out of Cairo was the first to con-
tain language that seemed to be aimed at encouraging abortion on demand, euthanasia, and same-sex marriage. The Beijing Conference built on the foundation of the Cairo
declaration and carried its concepts further. The Beijing Conference not only underscored Cairo's population control concepts but also sought to end all "abuse" of women. Abuse of
course, is rightfully condemned and can never be justified. The
Beijing Conference, however, endorsed a very broad notion of
what constitutes "abuse." The Beijing Platform for Action, for
example, contended that women could only meet their highest

and best use when employed outside the home, and it urged the governments of the world to establish day care centers that would free women from the servitude of children and families. Beijing's conclusions demanded sponsored and controlled day care for children, no restrictions of any kind on abortion, and quotas for women in government.

Perhaps most pernicious of all was the definition of "gender" as a "social construct" with no connection to biology. Participants at the Beijing Conference had suggested that there are at least five genders and had left the door open for further "social construction."

The plan was to have the stated goals of the Beijing Conference brought to fruition at the Istanbul Conference. Cairo had introduced the concepts, Beijing had defined and amplified them, and now, here at Habitat II, the objectives were to be tied to an agenda that actually might lay conditions on members of the international community.

The drafts of the proposed agenda that had come out of the PrepComs included language that was subtle and broad— written more to rule out objections to the Beijing goals than to state the goals themselves. But small numbers of vigilant PrepCom participants who disagreed with the Beijing objectives had recognized the potential pitfalls in certain of these broad paragraphs and had "bracketed" them.

Brackets are an interesting device in the adoption of UN declarations. UN documents are generally adopted by "consensus" rather than by vote. The advantages of this system are obvious. No nation has to go on record as having been firmly on either side. The procedure both exploits and accommodates the desire of most nations to be cooperative and make friends.

In the PrepComs there exists an opportunity to point out the language that will restrain the delegates from reaching consensus. That language is then "bracketed" so that compromise language can be found and consensus can still be achieved.

Whereas alert participants in the PrepComs had located the permissive paragraphs, it was our job to convince the delegates not to simply remove the brackets, as many Western countries wanted to do. Our goal was to encourage the delegates to demand that different and more limited language be substituted for the offending (bracketed) paragraphs and to withhold consensus until that language was changed. That withholding is trickier than it sounds. In Cairo, for instance, consensus was declared even though twenty-three nations had recorded their reservations in writing. The chairman of the drafting committee has the power to simply declare consensus after hearing only the speakers he chooses to call upon. Withholding consensus, therefore, requires some aggressiveness.

As an attorney I was expected to author, or at least oversee the creation of, some of the more limited language desired from the point of view of the Caucus for Stable Communities, the caucus of which United Families was a member.

✳

Before Richard could do anything else, however, he had to make good on his promise of copies of his paper to large numbers of delegates. It took only a short while to become familiar with the copy machines available, but using them was expensive—many times the cost that Richard was used to paying for copies. His paper was not as long as legal publications often tend to be, but even a sixteen-page piece was an expensive undertaking when meeting such a large number of requests. Richard quickly depleted almost all of the cash he had brought with him. Withholding enough only for absolute emergencies, he still had made only a dent in the demand for copies. He finally learned of a machine that would operate with a credit card, but when he ran his card through the magnetic reader it was not accepted.

Richard quickly did some arithmetic in his head. The airline ticket. The rugs. He had gone over his limit. It was more annoying than embarrassing. He went to find a telephone with which he could make an international call.

The bank of phones at the Hilton was in a lobbylike place with windows to the outside. It was perhaps the most pleasant place in the hotel. Richard called the number that was listed on the back of his credit card and asked to talk with someone about extending his credit limit. A personable young woman answered: "Certainly, Mr. Wilkins. How much would you like?"

"A thousand dollars," he answered, without bothering to calculate his needs. Surely $1,000 would be plenty. It discouraged him to have to spend the money in this way. Nevertheless, the paper was affording him conversations with many of the delegates, and he decided it was worth it. He determined not to worry about the money.

All day long Richard talked with delegates about his paper. He wasn't sure whether he was having an impact. Delegates were noncommittal, but definitely interested. Their questions were searching and thoughtful. They taxed Richard's limited research, but, somewhat to his surprise, he was able to answer every inquiry.

Wednesday evening, after dinner, Richard gathered with Susan and others from the Caucus for Stable Communities in Susan's tiny room at the Ulubat. Susan had brought with her a special transformer that emitted a rather odd smell when plugged into the hotel electrical socket. The transformer made it possible to run the desktop computer and a full-sized laser printer that she had also brought. That first night when Richard saw all of her equipment he was astonished. "I just went down to K Mart," Susan said, "and got some big plastic storage boxes and packed it all up the best I could. I knew I was risking a lot, but I was sure we'd need it all." She was, of course, right. So they all sat around Susan's computer, with their noses full of the odor from her transformer, and labored over the bracketed sections of the proposed agenda, desperately trying to avoid dangerously broad language that could harm families without appearing to ask for too much.

So passed those first two days after Richard's talk at the Forum: days of lobbying, and nights of writing.

While Richard and Susan were involved in these activities, the other members of United Families International were also busy. Back at the NGO Forum they were manning a booth, dispensing information, and hoping for visits from people with green badges.

The NGO Forum was composed of booths and workshops put on by literally thousands of nongovernmental entities who wished to influence the outcome of the UN conference. The Forum was a marketplace, often raucous, of competing views. It was in this turbulent world that most of my fellow residents of the Ulubat worked.

On Thursday afternoon the United Families booth received a visitor. It seems the man had earlier picked up some of the United Families literature, having caught the booth unmanned. He returned that afternoon to ask a question that the brochures did not answer.

"By any chance," he asked, "are you members of The Church of Jesus Christ of Latter-day Saints?" Sue Barton, the

---

United Families person at the booth, told him that although they were not attending as members of the Church, it was indeed true that all of them were Latter-day Saints.

"Allow me to introduce myself," he said in British-sounding English. "I am Johnson N. Mwara, the elders quorum president in Nairobi, Kenya. I am a member of the committee to choose ten people from NGOs to speak to Committee One before the final drafting of the Agenda is accomplished. Do you have a spokesperson that you would like to nominate?"

Sue replied quickly that their spokesperson was Richard Wilkins, a law professor from BYU, whose remarks he may have heard on Tuesday night. She gave Richard an enthusiastic endorsement and said that yes, indeed, they would like to have him nominated to speak.

At this reply Brother Mwara looked at his watch and noted that he had only a few minutes before the closing of the nominations, and he hurried off to place Richard's name in consideration. Richard would be nominated to represent the Caucus for Stable Communities inasmuch as a nominee had to represent a whole caucus, not just a member organization like United Families.

All of the group had known since early Wednesday that certain NGO speakers would have the opportunity to speak to the full meeting of Committee One. There had been much buzz about who among the thousands there might receive the nod. It was not something that had been done at other UN conferences. Normally the Forum, together with whatever lobbying efforts could be managed, was the extent of the NGO influence. But at this particular conference the official deliberations had been divided into Committee One and Committee Two. For the most part the same delegates sat on both committees, wearing first one hat and then the other. Committee One was to gather information from those so eager to give it, and then Committee Two was to meet to draft the document, at the end of the information-gathering stage.

There was considerable wondering about why this new Committee One and Committee Two format had been introduced at this conference. Rumors around the Forum had it that Bella Abzug, the chair of the Women's Caucus, had used her considerable influence to get the formation of Committee One at this all-important conference so that she could have a formal platform. The grapevine also held that she had engineered these ten speaking slots and intended to have them all for members of the Women's Caucus. If it truly was all the invention of Ms. Abzug, it turned out to be more than she bargained for.

Sue Barton could hardly wait to inform us that I had been nominated to speak at the Plenary Session of Committee One. "Of course there are lots of people nominated. Brother Mwara said that there would be tryouts among the nominees, so you still might not make it. But it's good even to be nominated, isn't it?"

While Sue was somewhat unsure as to whether I would, in the end, speak to the Plenary Session, I knew instantly that I would. I sloughed it off a bit to the others and behaved as if I wasn't expecting to be selected, but I knew that I would be, just as surely as if it had already been decided. And I knew something else. I knew that the time up until the Monday talk would be among the most difficult in my life.

When I could break away I got to a telephone and talked with Melany. I told her all my feelings and the foreboding that accompanied them. It was intensely real and frightening. Melany's love comforted me as always. I was stronger after the call.

✳

The tryouts were planned for Saturday morning. All day Friday and Friday night the group around Susan's computer was devoted to making suggestions as to just the right words for Richard to say at the tryouts. He would have only about two minutes, and it was important that they be used effectively.

The Caucus for Stable Communities had, of course, already made some nominations. They had designated some high officials of the Catholic Church who were their preferred representation. Now, thanks to Johnson Mwara's intervention, the Caucus would also be nominating a supportive law professor. They were happy to have another possibility, but to be awarded one of those final ten speaking slots was beyond their realistic expectation anyway. The Caucus just hoped for the best.

Richard couldn't tell any of the others what he was certain of in his heart, and he carried the burden of it. Twice on Friday he called Melany for comfort. She accepted what he said on face value and only reassured him that whatever the difficulties might be, he would be made equal to them.

He was told to be at the Hilton for tryouts at ten on Saturday morning. As a theater person it should not have unnerved him, but under the circumstances it did. And just what were those circumstances exactly? He wasn't even sure of that. He only knew that they hung heavily over his head. Friday night he had particular trouble getting to sleep on his little platform. He struggled to understand his anxiety and finally decided that what he was feeling was a concentrated responsibility.

It was the United States Constitution that gave Richard his grasp of what he was feeling. That might seem to others an unlikely place to seek understanding, but Richard had an attachment to the Constitution—the kind that some might have to a favorite melody or a piece of precious poetry. He loved it. Its language was delicious to him, and more than once it had helped him to have perspective about things of import in his life.

"We the people . . ."

Richard was fond of reminding students of the utter genius of beginning the Constitution with these three words. "It's the people who create the federal government. It's the people who create the *power* of governments."

Some very conservative folks really get it wrong. They have the notion that somehow the states give the power to the federal government. Wrong! It's the people. The idea of its being the states who give power to the federal government is a theory rejected by those first three words. "We the people . . ." Not we the thirteen colonies, or we the fifteen states, or we the fifty states. It's "we the people."

Richard loved to think about the genius of it. He cherished it. "We the people . . ."

But the United Nations has *only* its sovereign nation members. It has no "we the people." "Clearly," Richard thought as he shifted his position on his platform, "that's what's wrong!" The United Nations is so valuable, so useful as an international forum for intergovernmental issues, but not as a potential source of governmental power, because it's not a representative democracy. The only tie to the people is that their sovereign nations are participating in it. It has no grass roots. The idea of the United Nations governing individuals is the very theory that the United States Constitution rejects as a way to govern.

But the United Nations *is* trying to govern. "So in a way," Richard thought, "the nongovernmental organizations are trying instinctively to correct a defect in the UN organization and operation. The NGOs are trying to be the grassroots."

Richard was not comfortable with it at all, considering the import it gave to his duty to speak, but he could see that it was true. Nongovernmental organizations were as close as the United Nations would ever come to "we the people." The responsibility was heavy. Too heavy. He was going to speak, and he needed to do it to represent millions of people.

As clearly as Richard could see the importance of the United Nations in transnational issues, he could see its inadequacy as a power to govern individuals. But it was the system in which he found himself addressing how individuals should be governed. And notwithstanding the awesome magnitude of the commission, he could see, on that anxious Friday night, that *he* and the other NGO laborers were trying to function as "we the people."

With his duty clear, he could pray for strength to perform it. Then he slept.

CHAPTER 5

Confronting the Women's Caucus

Richard arrived at the auditorium half an hour early. It was already a buzz of activity. He inquired, and learned that he would be tryout number 39. He would have some time to wait, it appeared. He sat himself down, and very soon a red-badged woman he hadn't met before approached him. Richard rose in his place and extended his hand. "I'm Richard Wilkins."

"Yes, I know," the woman responded. "I caught your talk on Tuesday night. Excellent. You've got it exactly right." Richard opened his mouth to say thank you, but the woman kept talking. They shook hands and she sat down next to him.

"People are always saying to me: 'Why do you bother with all these meetings? These documents don't have any teeth. The United Nations doesn't have any jurisdiction; there's no authority behind any of these documents.' But I always answer: 'They don't need teeth. They don't need authority.'" She moved her head toward Richard and closed one eye as if she were about to share a great secret. "I say: 'They've got *influence!* That's where the power is—it's in the *influence*, the influence and the purse strings.'" She paused for a second or two, but it was clear she didn't expect a response yet. She went on.

"Influence is always more powerful than control. It's the power of words and the power of money. The people here at the UN write these documents and then, before very long, the ideas in these documents are acceptable, because—well, here they are in this UN document, so they must be okay. Then the ideas get tied to programs that bring money into a country, and *voila!* The ideas have got their toehold. These documents come into domestic governments through the back door—they're just all of a sudden part of things and people take 'em for granted. They must be legitimate because the United Nations says so. Human beings are funny. They don't even remember they ever felt differently. Unquestionably, the power is in the *influence*. And the influence is in the words and the purse strings."

The woman had probably been saving up this response since Tuesday night. Richard let her continue.

"In our country right now the politicians that have control are big advocates of some of these things that came out of Cairo and Beijing—so they're speeding up the cycle of the influence coming in; but fast or slow, the influence still bears fruit. The only difference is in the pace of the process. No doubt about it! The real power is in the influence."

There was a short pause and Richard interjected what seemed vaguely like an appropriate reaction. "The pen is mightier than the sword," to which the woman responded, "Yep, especially when the pen writes both the words and the checks."

Richard looked up to the stage at the UN officials in charge. They were somewhat huddled, and it occurred to Richard that something might be brewing, but the thought was short-lived and unimpressive. As quickly as it arose it was gone.

The woman kept talking. "Everyone always wonders how these social engineers got to have so much muscle around here. But, you know, the UN has been that way since the beginning. Everything you read—these elite intellectuals that want to rearrange the world according to what they think is 'rational' have had the clout around here for fifty years. That's why the world has gone so far in that direction. Influence. The *words*. The *purse strings*. No indeed, teeth just aren't necessary."

Richard recognized the frustration he was hearing in the woman's tone. He was beginning to find it familiar. It came out time and again in NGO advocates for the traditional family. How do you fight the impact of a philosophy that has invaded the international thought process like an invisible toxin, slowly smoking its way into our civilization with condescension for people trying to live the way the prophets have taught? Isaiah knew what he was talking about when he warned us of the dangers of calling evil good and good evil (see Isaiah 5:20). Common sense, Richard thought, is uncommon indeed. "Studies show . . ." was the byword here, and what the studies showed most often and most clearly was that research was being oddly weighted and evaluated in irregular and prejudicial ways.

"A fellow named Allan Carlson over at the Howard Center for Families and Religion got me turned on to looking at some of the UN history. Fascinating guy. Anyway, Carlson has been particularly interested in Alva Myrdal. She was one of the heavy hitters in the late forties and fifties. She came in as the principal director of the United Nations Department of Social Welfare in 1949. Then from '51 to '55 she was director of the UNESCO Department of Social Sciences. Alva Myrdal. She's a Swede. Ever heard of her?"

Richard acknowledged that he had, but beyond that he recalled nothing.

"Ol' Alva was a social engineer that took it to a whole new level! Even recommended eugenics to eliminate what she called 'worthless individuals' from the population."[4] She was extreme all right!

Richard felt a chill as his mind was filled with all the scriptures that warned against denigrating the worth of souls (see D&C 18:10; Mosiah 28:3, 4). He commented only that he understood Sweden had adopted some of that social policy at one point.

"Yeah! Well, she was the one that designed it. I told ya she was a heavy hitter.

"Anyway, when she was heading up Social Sciences at UNESCO she had the purse strings for a bunch of money. And she had these radical ideas and she funded universities with UN grants to sponsor professors and students who went along with her far-out beliefs. So now it's a generation later, and the kids that were trained in the universities that got those grants are all grown up. And we've got all these people running around here that were fed on her ideology and supported by UN dollars.

"No question. Alva Myrdal understood about influence.

"She used to say that she wasn't a socialist because she didn't want to control the means of production. But that was only true because she thought it was too complex and unnecessary. She thought it was easier—and more effective in terms of regulating the way children are raised—to control *consumption* instead. One incredible line in one of her books (I still can't get over how blatant it is) said: 'What people with children do with their incomes should no longer be considered a matter exclusively of individual liberty.'[5] Boy, I tell ya, it gives me the creeps. Makes me feel like a little tin figure that she wants to play life with." The woman closed her eyes and affected a little shudder, but her pause did not last long.

"Another thing Carlson turned me on to was reading the books that Alva's kids wrote. I wanted to see what made her tick, so I read a couple of the books by her son and one by her daughter. The son's books were, well—mostly vitriol there. Ya tend to discount some of it, because he hates her. 'Course, she wasn't much of a mother. The remarkable book was by her daughter. She's certainly sympathetic to her mother, but in spite of herself she ends up being the one that exposes the real Alva Myrdal." The woman shook her head slowly as if she were rereading in her mind the engrossing background she had gleaned from Alva Myrdal's daughter. She intended no response from Richard and she received none.

"Alva herself was raised in an offbeat home environment. She even called her childhood 'hellish.'[6] Her father was an atheist and a social activist. There were a lot of those around in the late nineteenth century. Anyway, Alva's mother had a hang-up about germs, so she never kissed her children and generally avoided contact. Naturally, coming out of that anybody would be a bit odd. Actually . . ." The woman stopped in mid-sentence and looked Richard full in the face. "Oh, I'm sorry, I'm running on at the mouth here. I didn't mean to bore you." By now, however, Richard was fascinated. He knew little of the early UN people. "No, please go on. I'm not bored at all."

They both took a quick look at their watches. It was almost time to start, but not quite. Besides, there were signs that the meeting might be starting late. At least no gavel had as yet been raised.

"Well, Alva actually flirted with religion a bit in her late teens. Even was confirmed in the Lutheran Church. But she ended up with a kind of religion of her own. She believed in good and she believed in evil. In fact, she believed that life was a battle between the two—sort of like the Zoroastrians, but with a difference. She believed in a creative power she was willing to call God, but this 'God' was not the definer of 'good' in her value system. Or the definer of evil either, for that matter. She ended up as a 'rationalist.' So that's what defined good and evil for her: her faith was in rationalism. Now, keep in mind that her true 'religion' was that good should fight evil. So there she was, with religious zeal fighting for a good that was defined by—what else really? Her *self* and her scholar heroes. For all the fancy definitions of rationalism, in the end it has to be defined as what makes sense to the rationalist herself. Any way you slice it, it's man playing God—or in this case woman defining good herself—by her own sense of 'reason.'

"With Alva Myrdal the biggest good of all was to get women out of their traditional role. She thought women were of more value as economic units than they were in the home. Besides, she wanted them to be *'free.'* She was absolutely disdainful of the traditional role of women.

"Another big one was that she wanted the state to govern the family, to make it work, to civilize it. She wanted the state to have the right to order the lives of children. She didn't trust the family unit. It was too primitive for her taste.

"Well, now just look at what we have today. Fifty years later we have the legacy of Alva Myrdal and others like her. We're here fighting—trying to undo the damage done by them. We're trying to put our fingers in the dike because the traditional role of woman *has* been denigrated, and the state *is* imposing itself into family life. It's just what she wanted. What she talked about. It's the power of her words—and her money. Well, not really hers, but the UN money she controlled.

"We're here fighting against abortion on demand, not because she was pro-abortion—she wasn't—but because that's become the way to relieve women of the traditional role. Nothing else she thought would do it has worked 100 percent. This generation has followed her lead by believing that the greatest good to fight for is 'freeing' women from the traditional role. And abortion on demand seems to do that, so here we are.

"We're here talking about state-provided day care and about children's rights instead of parents' rights, because those are the ways to fight for her other great good: to put the state in charge of children.

"These causes are her definition of good. It's her agenda. And it came to fruition through UN documents and UN money. That's the way it is: the words and the pocketbook. The documents and the purse strings.

"You talked the other night about how these things inevitably shape the norms and become the international custom. Well, the norms and customs we're dealing with right now were shaped half a century ago. And they were shaped by the United Nations with major input from a kid raised in an atheist home, without a mother's physical affection, and who grew up, according to her daughter, envying men but unwilling to sacrifice the full gratification of her female sexuality. I'll tell you her family paid the price. She thought she was 'having it all,' but she didn't really. And truth is, *we're* paying the price as well. The price of her 'rational' influence. Incredible! Truth is stranger than fiction. If Gulliver were to look in on us today, he'd see we're all ruled by Houyhnhnms after all."

The gavel was coming down. The woman was silent. Richard had only a moment or two to think about what his rather uncommon companion had said. Perhaps her premise had truth in it. Influence is certainly the great power. And if it is extended by self-interested rationalism, the potential for blunder takes on mammoth proportions. Reason is indeed a product of man's own thought and is therefore hazardously subject to error. Some truths, apparently, are simply not unfailingly self-evident. What a source of reassurance it is that we have scriptures and we have a prophet. Richard, for his part, had always known that no mortal intellect is self-sufficient.

Nevertheless he felt a renewed determination that, whatever he would say in these UN assemblies, he had better be true to a source of truth over and above his own perception.

The gavel was coming down again. It was difficult to call the meeting to order. The room, by now, was filled with three hundred nominees, each hoping to receive one of those ten speaking slots. Richard realized that number 39 was not such a late call number after all.

Finally the chairman of the meeting was speaking. He explained the method that had been set up to choose from among the three hundred nominees and then indicated his desire to begin the process.

Procedures to select the NGO speakers had been developed by the International Facilitating Group (IFG), an organization that coordinates NGO efforts at UN conferences. The system was approved by Working Committee One—the committee that had been formed for the first time at Habitat II to hear the NGO input.

The arrangement of the "tryouts" was to have those nominated to speak each deliver a two-minute talk. A panel of judges was to decide from those auditions which of the speakers would receive the coveted ten slots to speak to the Plenary Session on Monday morning. There were seven judges, and one of them was serving as chair of the "tryouts."

When the meeting began I looked at the large number of nominees and realized that there would be no chance of being finished in time to join my United Families associates at a picnic they were planning with the Istanbul Branch of the Church. I was disappointed. It sounded like a respite that would have served me well as I prepared for a couple of difficult days. I still had no question at all that I would receive one of the slots. Nor had the certainty left me that I would have a challenging time while I awaited the opportunity.

No sooner had the chairman indicated his desire to begin than a member of the Women's Caucus rose to her feet and demanded the floor. She was familiar to Richard. She was one of the women who had confronted him after his speech the previous Tuesday night. Both her expression and her tone were much the same as they had been when he had first encountered her. It was clear that she was not in a pleasant frame of mind.

"I protest! I am here to proclaim this entire selection procedure invalid. As the most important NGO participant at Habitat II, the Women's Caucus has the unquestionable right to control 80 percent of the official presentation time."

She was simply declaring that because of the power and prestige of the Women's Caucus they were entitled to at least eight of the ten slots.

"The Women's Caucus will choose who is going to address this plenary session. We have really organized this whole meeting. We know what are the issues of concern to the world. We are the only ones qualified to give any real input into this meeting, because this meeting wouldn't have happened without us!"

Oh, really? Was this an announcement that the scuttlebutt around the Forum had been true? Was it the Women's Caucus that had come up with this whole idea? Indeed, was it the Women's Caucus that was responsible for the very formation of this "Committee One"? It was not too far-fetched to believe it possible. They were definitely the largest and the best organized of all the groups there, and the UN did have a long history with them. But did they honestly have the power to format the meeting of the delegates? That seemed to be what the spokeswoman was claiming.

There was disorder and noise everywhere. The chairman gaveled it down: "I, too, protest. We have been charged by the International Facilitating Committee and by the Working Committee Two to select a diverse range of NGO views on a variety of topics, and we propose to make those evaluations and selections today."

The woman was angry at his lack of acquiescence.

"No man has the right to evaluate what a woman has to say!"

Thereupon ensued one of the most bitter and irrational rhetorical battles I have ever witnessed. When the IFG-appointed panel pointed out that the selection procedures had been established long before Habitat II and with the approval of the Women's Caucus, the Women's Caucus responded that rules should never get in the way of justice. When other NGOs protested that the claimed right to eight speakers would preclude presentations of other viewpoints, the Women's Caucus retorted that the objection was irrelevant because the Caucus's outlook was more important than other possible opinions. When others pointed out that the Caucus would likely receive the majority of the speaking slots simply because of the sheer number of their nominees, the Caucus replied that it was unwilling to leave that outcome to chance.

For almost three hours the bitter battle continued, each claim more preposterous than the one before it. Richard sat there and listened, dumfounded. With the others he issued an occasional audible manifestation of his shock. More often he was simply openmouthed with a gaping stare at the arguments being made by the Women's Caucus.

The contention on the floor kept escalating. From moment to moment Richard expected someone to stop it. It plainly shouldn't have been allowed. Finally he could stand it no longer. He stood and began to shout out a request for the floor: "Mr. Chairman! Mr. Chairman," he said. And again: "Mr. Chairman." He thought he could be heard over the din, but there was so little sense of order that it hardly mattered. "Mr. Chairman," he tried again. He persisted. Six times. Seven. Eight. At last he was recognized.

"I am an American. I have been a law professor for twelve years and never have I heard arguments that had such little appeal to either a rule of law or a sense of justice. There are limited speaking slots available and procedures to select a broad range of speakers have been in place and approved for some time. Now the Women's Caucus appears and claims that because of its size and power it is entitled to disregard those rules. This is quite like a litigant coming into a courtroom and declaring that, because of her wealth and prestige, she is entitled to her own brand of justice. Law and justice should treat everyone equally and fairly."

Richard went on to talk of the absurdity that the Women's Caucus should complain so loudly when five of the seven on the selection committee were hand-chosen by the Caucus itself. Their input was already disproportionate.

"It's time to turn this attempt aside and get on with the established procedures!"

Richard sat down. He was flush with the release a person feels after bursting out of a gate where he has been constrained too long. It took a moment before he realized that he was receiving a standing ovation. The representative of the Women's Caucus turned on her heels and left the meeting. Everything was changed.

In the hours that followed, Richard watched the tryouts with half attention. The woman next to him was still talkative from time to time, and generously admiring of Richard's assertive statement, but she was courteous enough not to be a steady stream of conversation. Richard didn't lack for the pensive time he always values—time to monitor the nuances around him.

He watched the judges on the panel. They seemed content, even pleased, that the process was proceeding and the ugliness ended. Most of them smiled at Richard when they caught his eye. It seemed an unlikely turn of events that they should be approving of Richard, a majority of them being representatives of the Women's Caucus. But as he returned their smiles and nodded politely, Richard came to understand that this was a small moment of glory for them—a moment that the leadership of the Women's Caucus had tried to take from them. Richard had, as it were, helped to reinstate the panel's authority. They were "somebody" again. Ah, how fickle human nature makes us!

Richard did not spend much time grieving for the picnic he was missing that afternoon. In fact, he soon forgot about it altogether. He enjoyed his sociable seatmate and was particularly amused when the woman occasionally inserted quotes from Myrdal and her children into the intervals between auditions. The excerpt Richard liked the best was actually from Alva's son. It was something about it being better to learn nature's laws and follow them instead of being forced to follow their requirements resisting and struggling—kicking like a small child.[7]

When Richard got back to the Ulubat it was midnight. He was tired, but this part was over. The news that he had been selected was waiting for him at the hotel desk when he arrived.

NOTE

The extended conversation in chapter 5 is a compressed composite of discussions Richard had with a variety of people during the course of his learning about the history and inner workings of the United Nations. The synthesis is provided here for the reader's benefit. All other events described in that chapter, as well as in the rest of the entire book, are exact accountings, with quotes word for word according to Richard's memory.

CHAPTER 6

A Prayer in the Night

Richard's instructions were for him to be at the Hilton
Hotel Sunday morning at eleven for a final meeting with the
International Facilitating Committee and the others who had
been selected to speak on Monday. The timing was awkward. If
he went to sacrament meeting he would have to leave that
meeting early and, of course, would miss the other meetings altogether. But Richard needed the sacrament. And he needed a
Sabbath—limited as it would have to be. He joined his United
Families friends and went to church.

The meetings were held in the apartment of a missionary
couple. Richard's eye went immediately to the Turkish rug on
their floor. It was beautiful—better quality, he could tell, than
those he had purchased. It occurred to him that they had
probably driven a better bargain as well. He had a moment of
struggle with the tenth commandment.

The apartment was good-sized and bright but not really
equipped to handle so many visitors. It was obvious, however,
that the extra worshippers were not an unhappy circumstance.
The Saints rejoiced in one another, and for a moment Richard
remembered the picnic he had missed the day before. His
friends were anxious to have him share in the joy of Saturday's
bonding and there were introductions and handshakings all

around. The missionary couple looked familiar to Richard. As soon as he heard their name he knew why.

"Lofgren. Oh my! You're Jonathan Lofgren's parents, aren't you?" Jonathan was a young actor with whom Richard and Melany had worked at the Hale Theater in Orem. The affection for Jonathan was quickly transferred to his parents, and the small Mormon world served Richard's need for warmth and connection on this shortened Sabbath morning.

The meeting began, but concentration was difficult. Richard, still filled with a spirit of foreboding, gave his entire effort to prayer and to the sacrament. The remarks of the speakers were less distinct in his mind. Richard remembers now only the honor felt in this tiny branch to have Elder and Sister Didier present and the love that all felt from one another.

I took a cab back to the Hilton and arrived just in time for the meeting. In contrast to the day before, the group seemed small. There were observers present—mostly, I noticed, from the Women's Caucus—but the Committee and the two handfuls of speakers were predominant.

The chairman made a few comments. He told us that there were still some questions about the fairness of the selection process and that it was possible that other speakers might be added, but his comments were somewhat confusing. At the time I didn't think anything was going to interfere significantly with the planned procedure. We were given brief instructions. Each of us was to be assigned to a room in which we would find computers—one for each of the people assigned to that room. We would be given four hours in which to write our talks, following which we would each be given a training session with a speech coach from a New York school of drama—whom, they made clear, they had flown in at great expense. The addresses, they said, were to be broadcast on American television, and it was important that we make every effort to be camera worthy. After all my years in the theater I was finally to have an experience with someone from a New York drama school. That part, at least, was attractive to me.

Richard entered the room to which he was assigned. The room was relatively long but quite narrow and felt closed in—crowded even. It was furnished with four desks, two of which were topped with computers. He was shown to one of the computers and a woman from Saudi Arabia was shown to the other. He recognized the woman from the auditions the day before. She was a Muslim, he remembered, and had an agreeable manner that was both gentle and intelligent. They took time for only a short conversation. She told him that she would speak about the role of women in Islam. It distressed her that the world looked upon Muslim women as oppressed and mistreated, a notion which she clearly did not feel accurately described her own situation or that of other contented Muslim women she knew. Richard found that fascinating and would have liked to hear her comments right there and then, but the clock was ticking away.

He turned on his computer and waited for it to boot. He sat with a hand on the mouse and watched the images slowly move toward readiness. As he was so engaged, some women entered the room. They wore red badges. Richard could easily read their identification because the women came and perched on the desk next to him—uncomfortably close. They were representatives of the Women's Caucus. His eyes avoided their stare, but their presence interrupted Richard's thought process and his hand fell off the mouse into his lap.

These rooms were supposed to be occupied exclusively by those designated to speak at the Monday session and the green-badged officials who were in charge. Richard's first thought was to wonder how the women had gained access. Then he thought about what the chairman had said that morning. If the Women's Caucus was still having success in questioning the selection process—well, then its political power was probably plenty strong enough for its members to be allowed free movement. He supposed that it was likely they could come and go as they pleased. It was no doubt naïve for him to have thought otherwise.

The staring women unnerved him. His hands were still in his lap and he was now looking steadily at the booted but empty monitor. The women simply stood and watched him. It wasn't until he put his hands on the keyboard that the women began a conversation in full voice:

"Can you believe that someone is going to talk about the traditional *family?*"

"That outmoded oppressive institution that's been responsible for every war since the beginning of time? How could *anybody* defend the *family?*"

"I can't imagine! And they're going to come out against same-sex marriage, as well! Can you believe it?"

"No, I can't. I thought surely we'd come to a point in civilization where we were rid of all discrimination. How could anyone be so full of hate that they wouldn't allow people who love one another to commit to one another?"

Richard's hands were tensed at the keyboard. He couldn't be sure if the women intended to divert him with debate or with intimidation. If it was debate, . . . well, he was not going to rise to it. He stayed silent. But the intimidation was working. He couldn't write. He couldn't even think.

The three women continued in conversation for several minutes until two of them bid their farewells and disappeared, leaving the one, still perched on the desk, watching Richard and the woman from Saudi.

It probably should have occurred to Richard that he and the Islamic woman were equally offensive to the Women's Caucus. He perhaps also should have noticed that the only two speakers who were to speak in defense of traditional ways of life were there, together, in that unpleasant narrow space, separated from the others. But it didn't occur to him. He didn't notice. Nor did he comprehend, at first, that whatever the intended effect of their monitoring, the presence of the women was planned, and would continue for the entire four hours. Every half an hour or so there was a kind of changing of the guard. When the replacement arrived there would be a few minutes more of the same type of conversation that the three women originally held. And always in full voice.

The woman from Saudi must have kept writing. Richard was unaware. An hour passed. Two hours. He had three sentences on his screen and they were awkward sentences at that. He put his head in his hands and then put his hands back to the keyboard. Nothing. His head ached. No, not just his head—every part of him. Had there been a brownout? Was it getting dark in the room, or was it only that his eyes were aching, too? He didn't know. He couldn't be sure of anything. It was like descending into a whirlpool of very black water. Destruction was the sure end of it. There was terror—not that he would die, but that he would cease to exist. Evaporate. Vanish. And it wasn't just horror at what *might* happen, but at what *was* happening. There was present agony. It was unlike anything Richard had ever endured.

I have argued eight cases before the United States Supreme Court. I know what pressure is. Ask any attorney who has had that privilege and he will tell you—it is the ultimate test of a lawyer's advocacy and is always accompanied by abject fear. It is a trepidation beyond the most anxious stage fright that I have ever felt. Richard Nixon said of himself that he had never known true terror until he argued a case before the Supreme Court. Later, he became president of the United States, he had difficult press conferences, but arguing a case before the Supreme Court was still the most terrifying moment of his life. I know what he means. Yes, I know what pressure is.

And I know what persecution feels like. I have given speeches that have evoked booing and hissing from the floor, and I have been vilified in the national and international press.

The feeling that day was not just pressure. It was not just persecution. It was a blackness of immense proportions that I have not experienced before or since.

✶

From somewhere deep in the vortex that was his heart at that moment, Richard suddenly thought of Melany. If he could just talk to Melany! If he could only feel her love! And he must have felt enough of it to give him some small strength, because he gradually became free to move. With great effort he pulled himself up from his chair and went out into the hall. He went to that pleasant lobby where the telephones were and looked outside into the sunlight. It occurred to him that it was not daylight in Utah. Melany would be in bed. But he had to call. He just had to. What's more, he knew that Melany would want him to. That knowledge was part of the strength that had brought him out to the phones in the first place. He picked up the phone.

Melany answered quickly and almost brightly. She always woke up that way. Ever since the children were little.

"Richard," she said, after he had haltingly told her of his troubled state, "do you have that copy of the Proclamation on the Family with you?"

"Yes, I think so. I'm sure I do. It's in my briefcase. It's been there all week."

"Get it out, dear. Read it. That's what you need to say in your talk. There's always safety in the prophet's words, Richard. Your security is in the Proclamation on the Family. If you use the Proclamation, you'll know you're doing what your Father in Heaven wants you to do. And that will bring you peace. I know it will. It always has. You've always been able to do the tough things when you know they're right, Richard. You can do it now, too."

Melany had provided a roadmap and a vote of confidence. The pain was easing.

"Richard, I'll pray for you, dear. It must be terrible to be going through this. What courage it must take! I'll pray for you to have the courage. I love you, Richard. I love you so much. I'll pray for you.

"It's fast Sunday tomorrow, and I'll ask the whole ward to pray for you. Oh, I know you won't want them to know the details, dear, but I'll just tell them you are involved in something difficult in Istanbul and that you need their love and prayers. You know you'll have them. The ward loves you—just loves you."

He could tell that Melany was concerned about his dwindling four-hour writing time. She was ready to hang up as soon as he was sounding like himself. "I'll pray for you. I love you. Call me when it's over." And his lifeline was in place.

As he walked back to the room where the computer waited, Richard kept in his mind the image of Melany kneeling beside their four-poster bed in the middle of the night—praying for him. A prayer born of both love and faith. A prayer in the night that yielded strength to him on the other side of the world.

✷

When I got back to the room I was able to shut out every-thing else from my consciousness except the task before me. The first thing I did was to hit the backspace and wipe out the two or three sentences that I had written up to that point. I got out the Proclamation and said a very practical prayer. I said, "Okay, what's the message?" And I read carefully with great concentration.

Just like the Constitution, the first words set forth the most fundamental of principles: that prophets of God made this proclamation and that marriage between a man and a woman is ordained of God and that the family is central to the Cre-ator's plan. All of that right there in the first paragraph. I knew I couldn't just read the Proclamation. I couldn't give my talk in religious terms—at least, not right then, I couldn't. I've since grown more bold, but that day I wanted to extract what I could timidly say to this more secular group and still find secu-rity in staying true to the prophets' message. In the margin of my copy I wrote: Central to Community.

For each paragraph I outlined the central idea and wrote it in the margin. It should have been difficult because the Proclamation has no real excess verbiage, but it was not hard at all. My margin notes included: "Sanctity of Life," "Care of Children," "Successful Families." Some places I simply under-lined, and I put a circle around "law-abiding citizens wherever they live." The last two paragraphs I starred: "We warn that the disintegration of the family will bring upon individuals, communities, and nations the calamities foretold by ancient and modern prophets.

"We call upon responsible citizens and officers of government everywhere to promote those measures designed to strengthen and maintain the family as the fundamental unit of society."

The Proclamation was truth and it provided the answer.

✵

It swept over Richard like a wave of tranquillity. He had less than an hour left on the clock, but he knew that it would be enough. He began:

"It is a pleasure to address you on the subject of international law and the family. International law addresses the relationships between nations and peoples. The family is what deals with relationships between humans on their most basic level. . . ."

All of it came together, and Richard's fingers almost had a life of their own. The family was more than just something to preserve. It was the only place where the problems of society could be successfully addressed. He knew that. Prophets of God had met in council and had told him so. In addition, he had the most profound of witnesses that it was true.

His concentration was interrupted when he heard the representatives of the Women's Caucus asking the Saudi woman for a copy of her talk. With what he thought considerable strength of character, the woman told them that she didn't think she should have to do that. "Give us a copy of your talk, or you'll be cut," she was told. So she complied.

In a few minutes the women returned and with no fanfare told the Saudi woman that her topic was not "germane." She had been cut from the program. Richard thought she was probably as bewildered as she was disappointed, but she left quietly and Richard was alone in the room.

It was not long before the Women's Caucus people returned. This time they asked for a copy of Richard's remarks. He told them that he was not yet finished, but they said it didn't matter. "Give us a copy or you'll be cut." He, like the Muslim woman, complied. On a superficial level he worried that his topic would receive the same treatment hers had received, but even as that fear entered his mind he discounted it. He never seriously questioned his survival as a speaker.

His conviction made no sense. His topic was no more "germane" to the strategy of the Women's Caucus than the Saudi woman's was. Nevertheless, he had no genuine doubt that he would survive.

When the women returned it was to introduce the coach from the New York drama school, who would give Richard direction on how to present his remarks. Apparently he had not been cut. He would speak on Monday morning, just as he had been sure he would.

The session with the drama coach was disappointing. She had been given the copy of my speech and had read it. She didn't like it. She suggested some rewriting using more colorful language. She told me I should have concrete examples. Stories, she said, were what I needed. She also told me to use my hands more. Gestures apparently would have added some of the color I lacked. But after what I had been through, her criticism was only amusing. By the time I met with her there was nothing she could have said that would have mattered at all.

My talk was not going to be colorful, but it was going to be what prophets of God wanted proclaimed to "responsible citizens and officers of government everywhere." I was thoroughly confident in my choice of both content and language. I was ready for the morning.

CHAPTER 7

"Where Have You Been?"

Monday morning when Richard opened his scriptures he found himself turning again to Jonah, as he had done almost every morning during the previous week. He identified so closely with Jonah.

And why not? He had much in common with this proto-type of reluctant laborers. He had allowed himself to be thrown into the United Nations sea in an effort to quiet a tempest that others had felt while he slept. Struggling in the sea, he felt swallowed up in the belly of the big fish of destiny. This morning he would be vomited out onto dry land, where he would deliver the Lord's warnings as he understood them.

And it was the dry land of Asia Minor, only a few hundred miles from the actual ancient Nineveh, where Jonah himself had preached. Richard, too, would foretell of calamity if the Lord's ordained way was not followed. He couldn't help but fantasize how he would react if he met with repentance and was actually able to prevent the endorsement of society's destruction that the United Nations seemed ready to make. Knowing himself, he rather thought that his link with Jonah would be complete. He, too, would probably be annoyed if a turnaround made his alarm prove to be false.

"No danger, there," he said out loud. His experience that

past week had been unusual, it was true, but it had not really dissuaded him from his pessimistic cynicism. "Hope" was still not a part of his motivation.

His motivation may not have been hopeful, but it was sure. He readied himself to go to the Plenary Session. He would do his duty.

Richard worried a little about the condition of his suit and the fact that the man in the mirror seemed older and more tired than usual. Oh, well! It was almost time to board the UN shuttle for the Hilton Hotel.

The United Families people all made it a point to stop by and give encouragement to Richard before he left. They were proud of him, and their support was pleasing.

When Richard walked into the auditorium it was a formidable sight, filled as it was with delegates and ambassadors. He smiled at some few people he knew; waved at those even fewer whom he knew better; and took his seat. He was starting to be a little fearful. He had to keep reminding himself of the security he could take in the content of his remarks.

The green-badged man from Holland that had been in charge of Sunday's preparatory meeting took the podium. He was, apparently, serving as chairman of the entire event. He gaveled the meeting to order and waited for the quiet.

The Dutchman's first announcement was that there would be some unscheduled speakers added to the program. Eight of them, to be exact. He said that because of the additions it was likely that there would not be time for some of the scheduled presenters and that all of the speakers who did address the body would be limited to six minutes instead of ten. He listed the names of the unscheduled additions (all of them from the Women's Caucus) and took his seat.

Richard had been listed as the next to the last speaker. So

the plan was to squeeze him out, was it? He shook his head in disbelief. He went over the events of Sunday afternoon in his mind. Clearly sometime between the time that the Saudi woman was cut and the time that the Women's Caucus read Richard's remarks, they had determined to change their tactics. Very clever! Cunning, even! At least it relieved him of some of his nervousness. He sat and listened to the eight interlopers.

Each speaker echoed the one preceding her. The message was that the world's housing problems would disappear if certain criteria were met: First, women must make the important decisions regarding resource allocation. Men, they said, are incapable of making those decisions because they simply could never understand. Second, alternative forms of sexual partnerships must be recognized. Third, women must have ready access to pregnancy termination. And fourth, we must have government-sponsored day care.

Occasionally a woman would have a little different twist on the discussion. The representative of the International Association of College Women, for example, addressed the strain that conflicting demands of family and profession can put on a mother. She suggested that women could be freed from this conflict by a combination of twelve hours a day of government-sponsored day care, distribution of labor-saving devices, and a proliferation of fast food restaurants (so women could feed their children on the way home from day care).

Richard had a sickening image of children being fed French fried potatoes in the car on the way to day care; being picked up twelve hours later and eating hamburgers in the car on the way home; then going immediately to bed, where it would be difficult to fall asleep because Mother was using her new vacuum cleaner.

Just as he was decrying the whole picture he turned around and saw that the woman was receiving a thunderous ovation. He asked himself if the world had gone mad. The thought that household devices and hamburgers could solve the complex problems of society seemed ludicrous. He was saddened that the goal seemed to be not to raise children, but to escape from them. Richard remembered a quote from Alva Myrdal's book that his Saturday seatmate had recited to him: "To put it bluntly, children are cumbersome not only during working hours but also at night and on Sundays."[8]

When the eighth speaker had concluded and was seated, an hour and a half had passed. Not one of the participants had kept to the six-minute limit. Notwithstanding the lateness of the hour, however, the chairman rose again and announced that they would now hear from a distinguished guest that had not previously been announced. With much fanfare, he ushered Ms. Bella Abzug to the stand.

Ms. Abzug held forth for more than ten minutes. She extolled the importance of the views the conference had just heard. The Women's Caucus, she said, was uniquely situated to ensure enforcement of the agenda's mandates because of its size and resources. The ugly patriarchal traditions can and must be stamped out. The abuse and slavery of women must end. Oppressive religion must release its yoke.

Sometimes the language was remarkably familiar to Richard. He began to wish that his Book of Mormon was in his briefcase. He would have loved to look in Alma 30 and compare what he was hearing to the complaints of Korihor—word for word.

✵

Once, when I was a freshman at BYU, I had a Book of Mormon class from Truman Madsen. I remember his telling us that the story of Korihor was a testimony of the Book of Mormon because his arguments against the gospel were arguments used in our day, not in the days of Joseph Smith. At the time I had not heard the arguments used in any other context but Alma 30. Nevertheless, Brother Madsen's comment had stuck with me, I guess, because sitting in that auditorium in Istanbul I was suddenly aware of the striking familiarity of the arguments I was now hearing in a contemporary circumstance.

The insight came all at once. Delayed some quarter century from my freshman memory, it was a testimony to me as well. I was being told by these speakers from the Women's Caucus that women were in "bondage" to men because of the "foolish traditions of [the] fathers," and that men only wanted to, in Korihor's words, "glut [them]selves with the labors of [women's] hands," that women "durst not look up with boldness, and that they durst not enjoy their rights and privileges" (Alma 30:27).

✵

After the seemingly endless rhetoric that Richard had heard that day, he began to understand why Alma had chosen to strike Korihor dumb. The idea made him smile.

By the time Ms. Abzug had finished her remarks it was clear that there would be no time for the other participants at all. Even the time for questions from the floor would be limited. But as the chairman received the microphone from Ms. Abzug, a delegate from Algeria showed an amazing amount of courage. He raised a point of order.

"Mr. Chairman," he asserted, "we were to hear a variety of views from NGOs this morning, but this has been turned into a seminar on radical lesbian feminism. I want to know if other views are being foreclosed." It was a shocking statement. Before the chairman could summon up a response, a delegation from the Holy See quickly seconded the motion, and the chairman was forced to open the floor of the conference for comments.

In rapid succession a series of individuals stepped to the microphones. The delegates were quickly informed of the events of the past few days—events of which they had no knowledge prior to the objection of the Algerian delegate. The Saudi Arabian woman was one of those who sought the floor. She explained the way in which she had been excluded because her views were considered not suitable.

After the revelations, one man stood and up and told the chairman that he was guilty of corruption.

The room went quiet and the chairman was visibly angry. In a restrained and measured voice he said that he had never been guilty of corruption. "Nevertheless, it may be appropriate to hear the remaining speakers." He turned immediately to Richard and told him that he would be allowed to speak, but that he would be given only four minutes. At the end of four minutes the microphone would be turned off.

It couldn't have been scripted better. All eyes were on Richard. After two hours of monolithically acrimonious, "colorful" presentations—after the wind and the fire—came

Richard's soft and loving message. He spoke a few sentences urging the international community to close the gap between participation of the governed and the international government. He told them that the family was what would be governed by the documents produced at that conference, and that the voice of the family must therefore be heard. He told them that the family is where little boys and little girls learn to love one another, to serve one another, and to take responsibility for one another. It is where they learn to be strong and caring men and women, where they learn to be contributing citizens. Be careful, he told them, before you discard thousands of years of tradition. Do not do it quickly or without great care. The family is the basic unit of society. It is central to our communities. If our problems are to be solved, they are to be solved in the families of the world. Do not adopt policies that will lead to disintegration of our families. We must, instead, strengthen them.

As it happened, four minutes were enough. Like Gideon of old, who needed to pare his numbers in order for it to be clear that the Lord had blessed the men in their battle (see Judges 7:2), Richard, perhaps, would have found ten minutes "too many." Brevity, after excess. Love, after hatred. Those in the room who had ears to hear recognized the truth as it came from four minutes of doctrine as confirmed in a proclamation made by prophets of God.

The chairman's anger was increased at the obvious effect of Richard's remarks. When questions came from the floor, he gave unlimited time to members of the Women's Caucus; but he warned Richard every time he received a question that he must keep his response to a few seconds. Richard did so—and his cause did not suffer for it.

At the close of the meeting, Richard was thronged. Many of the delegates had tears in their eyes. If they had before felt that they could ignore UN documents, that seemed no longer possible.

A delegate from one of the Arab countries put his arms around Richard and asked him a question that was to haunt him for months: "Where have you been?" To have support for traditional families from a Western nation was more than the developing countries of the world could have hoped for. No matter that few of the American-based NGOs at Habitat II shared Richard's views. These delegates felt new hope that anyone from the Western world was on their side.

If Richard had been Jonah that morning, and a few moments before was Gideon, he was now more like Peter on the day of Pentecost, as the crowd of delegates around him asked the equivalent of "Men and brethren, what shall we do?" (Acts 2:37).

They really seemed willing to do whatever was necessary. They only needed help and support. Richard was shocked at the magnitude of the response. Before he thought what it would mean, he said: "I'll write something for you. I'll get it to you tomorrow." Could there really be hope this time? Maybe. Maybe. He was incredulous. But, maybe.

CHAPTER 8

The Parting of the Red Sea

"Melany, I gave the speech! Well, I didn't give 'the speech,' but I spoke. And Melany, it was unbelievable." The words tumbled out of Richard's mouth into the telephone. He told her of the tears and of the Arab who hugged him. He told of his promises to write something. "I'll be up all night writing, because I've got to have it ready by morning. It's sure a far cry from the kind of step-by-step writing and rewriting that I'm used to."

"Know what it reminds me of, Richard? It reminds me of when you were fifteen years old and working as a cub reporter for the *Deseret News*. You had to write quickly and concisely then, remember? Get the facts down on paper and have it ready for the deadline! I remember you loved it then. Well, here you are again. Seems like old times."

Richard remembered. "Actually, that was pretty good training for something like this."

All at once Richard noticed the date on a brass calendar in the lobby. It was the tenth of June, the night he had planned the roses and the party. The twenty-five red roses would still be delivered, but the rest of it wasn't going to happen.

"Closing night tonight. I wish I were there."

"Me, too. But let's not get melancholy. We're giving up a little romance, but we've traded it for a pretty profound kind of love, Richard. What you're doing in Istanbul is important. I'm proud of you."

When Richard hung up the telephone he felt that he could conquer the world, should it be required of him. All that *was* required of him, however, was to write something to help the delegates find a way to withhold consensus on the bracketed language. And that Monday, around Susan's odoriferous computer, Richard and Susan and Susan's son Bradley worked most of the night to produce a document that could encourage and enable the delegates to hold their ground in the final deliberations that would produce the Habitat Agenda.

When Richard arrived at the Hilton Hotel the next morning he was pleased with the night's labor. His document had been written quickly and concisely (just like those old days at the *Deseret News*), but they were all well pleased with it. It remained only for him to go back to the copy machines and then distribute it, both of which proved to be more difficult than one would expect.

Richard had made so many copies of last week's talk that he had completely exhausted the additional $1,000 credit limit he had arranged. Once again the copy machine would not take his MasterCard. He went back to the phones and called the number he had called the previous week. He was connected again to the same friendly woman. "How much would you like this time, Mr. Wilkins?" "Oh, I guess another $1,000." "Are you sure that will be enough?" "My goodness, I hope so!" "Very well. Go ahead and use your card right away. The extra limit has been applied."

Richard looked at his watch and realized that too much of the morning had gone by. He hadn't thought to take a list yesterday of those who wanted copies, so the distribution posed some problems. At least he had better hurry and get those copies made.

As Richard rounded the corner on the way to the copy machine, he almost collided with one of the Arab men who had spoken to him after his talk.

"Oh, Professor Wilkins, I have been looking for you. I wanted to know how to get a copy of the material you said you would prepare for us. The Islamic Conference is preparing a position paper and we would like to be sure that it will include your suggestions."

"I'm on my way to the copy machine right now," Richard responded. "This is the material I promised. Walk along with me and I'll give you the first copy." The two men were cordial to one another, but more formal than they had been the day before in the tender aftermath of Richard's remarks.

"We have a difficult task ahead if we hope to succeed in changing the bracketed material," the Arab said. "The West is firmly against us. The United States delegation, I understand, has received instructions not to come home unless the brackets are removed and the document remains as drafted."

Richard's heart fell. He knew the weight that course would carry.

"Who gave those instructions?"

"I don't know. I only know what has been told to us."

Richard fell silent. He was tired, having slept so little the night before, and this news deepened his fatigue. He had been so hopeful, but now—well, this was dreadful information. He made a few copies, said his thank-yous and his good-byes to the grateful beneficiary of his night's work, and hurried back to his United Families friends.

The United States delegation held a briefing every day, and that day Richard attended it. He asked if the "rumor" he had heard was true. Yes, it was, said Melinda Kimball, the head of the delegation. "Where did that instruction come from?" Richard asked. "Washington," was the response.

"Washington," he told the others. "That's all she knew. The word would have to come from the State Department, I suppose, but low level or high level?" Someone had the idea to phone Chris Smith, congressman from New Jersey, who was a friend. "He'll be able to find out." And Congressman Smith did find out. He called the State Department and asked where the directive had originated. "The White House," they said. Well, that was high level, all right.

Someone in the group had read an American newspaper that morning and said that it just didn't make sense. President Clinton had only that day signed the Defense of Marriage Act. So on the one hand he went on record opposing same-sex marriage, while the same day someone in his administration sent instruction that this influential UN document should preserve language favoring that "marriage." Richard felt he would never understand the purely political mind. His frustration was acute.

By the end of the day he had come to grips with the truth that the battle would be more formidable than he had before believed. Nevertheless, the support he was feeling also was strong. Many groups were asking for copies of the material he had helped put together Monday night, and there was talk of some of the coalitions planning to join in the recommendations. His hopes were not completely dashed. He left with the others for the Ulubat.

On a major arterial about a block from the UN compound, Richard and the others were met by a scene that disquieted them more than had the disconcerting news from the United States delegation. They saw several men cleaning the streets. At first they didn't realize what the men were mopping up from the pavement. They were horrified when they saw that it was blood. Lots of it.

They all knew that there was some political unrest in Turkey because of tension between the religious fundamentalists and the military regime. And there had been all the barbed wire and the machine guns around the Ulubat. But blood in the streets! How could the UN compound have been so insular that they didn't know what was going on outside? They all shuddered to think of what they might have encountered had they been a bit earlier.

The next morning the Hilton Hotel was buzzing with rumors about the incident: they said people were being gathered up and hauled off to prison; that NGO representatives were being arrested and taken away; that there were hundreds killed; there were a few killed; there were none killed because they used rubber bullets. Having seen the blood, of course, Richard seriously doubted the rubber bullets idea. Nevertheless, although many were eager to pass on the rumors, no one seemed to have any authoritative information. The episode caused everyone to be fearful of venturing outside of the UN compound.

But then, that Wednesday morning, things began to happen so quickly at the Habitat II Conference that very few were able to leave the compound, anyway. Certainly not Richard. He remained at the meetings for three days and three nights of frenetic effort. It was to garner and maintain support for changes in the Habitat Agenda. Richard had had his last night of sleep on his plywood platform at the Ulubat.

That Wednesday morning, the "Heads and Members of Arab Delegations Participating in the UN Conference" issued a statement—first in Arabic and then in English—which stated that they would sign no agenda that did not recognize the value of religious and cultural heritage, that did not recognize the family as the basic unit of society, that did not acknowledge that marriage consisted of a union between a man and a woman (not individuals of the same sex), and that failed to clarify that no nation had the obligation to provide abortion services, because the "fetus have [has] the full right to live and be raised according to religious and local norms."[9]

Later the G-77 nations, consisting of 139 African and Asian nations and the Pacific Rim states, plus China, took a similar stand: they would sign no agenda that did not preserve important local sovereign flexibility in implementing agenda goals, would not sign an agenda that recognized same-sex marriage and failed to recognize the importance of traditional families, and would not sign any agenda that required abortion on demand. That same day the United Kingdom, through its secretary of state for the environment, issued a strong and very persuasive statement urging the conference to reject the "culture of death."[10]

It was becoming clear, on that Wednesday of the second week of June, that the Habitat II Conference was in the process of being turned upside down.

If Richard had had the time to think, he probably would have stood in the middle of it all with his hands on his head. How could all this be happening? But everyone wanted to talk with him, get his ideas, and his approval. There wasn't time for reflection. Besides, down deep he knew how it was happening. It was a blessing. A blessing being given to the immense efforts of a relatively few people who were willing to work to bring about a marvel. Groups of Catholics and Muslims had been working hard ever since the Cairo Conference. Here in Istanbul the Goodmans, a family of singers who had come as part of the United Families contingent, had been giving concerts that warmed people's hearts. Workshops from other NGO participants had begged for this change of direction. Individuals who came to represent NGOs had spent untold hours giving very personal service to other attendees, never forgetting that they were there to urge love and mutual support. Now, this Wednesday, in a whirlwind, it appeared that all of it might work together for success. Every single contribution, every tiny step, seemed to have made a difference—in fact, an indispensable difference. And the Habitat II Agenda was going to be changed.

There were sections in the proposed Habitat Agenda where the broad language allowed interpretation that would support purposes and programs harmful to families. Rarely was the intent overtly stated. It was necessary for us to be familiar with what we came to call the "buzzwords" or "code" for the drafters. "The right to reproductive health," for instance, was code for abortion on demand. "The rights of the child" was no longer about a child's right to *protection,* but about the child's right to *choice.* Therefore, "the rights of the child" had become code for eliminating the rights of the parent.

Same-sex marriage was the objective behind several "codes." For instance, if the word "gender" could be substituted for the word "sex," then ultimately (they hoped) it could be accepted as Bella Abzug had already indicated, that

> the meaning of the word "gender" has evolved as differentiated from the word "sex" to express the reality that women's and men's roles and status are socially constructed and subject to change.[11]

If discrimination on the basis of "gender" could be condemned, therefore, same-sex marriage would have to be allowed. Another "code" was to stress in the documents that "various forms of the family exist," and that all forms deserve support.

Inasmuch as many of these codes and buzzwords are difficult to ferret out, our task was both to recognize the lurking pitfalls in the proposed agenda and to find a way to remove the negative potential with the smallest possible changes to the language. Grand and sweeping changes would have little chance of adoption, but a word or two here or there would be difficult for our adversaries to oppose without exposing their entire strategy. It was necessary, therefore, for us to be alert both legally and diplomatically.

The proposed wording in one paragraph, for example, was: "Crime prevention through social development is one crucial key . . ."

Since this would certainly be interpreted as an endorsement of social engineering by the state and a diminution of parental rights, the words "strengthening families and" were added just prior to the words "social development." This creates instead: "Crime prevention through strengthening families and social development is one crucial key . . ." which is quite a different meaning and only a small change in actual wording.

In another paragraph a list of people whose rights must be honored included children, women, and vulnerable groups. We did not challenge that existing list. We simply added "families" to the list—which again thwarted an intended move toward autonomy for children.

There were several pages of such suggested substitutes for the bracketed material. One change in particular we hoped for, however, was markedly offensive to the opposition. It was of the grand and sweeping variety that we tried to avoid, but there was no eluding the need for this one.

Paragraph 18 in the proposed agenda declared:

The family is the basic unit of society and as such should be strengthened. It is entitled to receive comprehensive protection and support.

(So far so good, but the next line is what makes the intent clear.)

In different cultural, political, and social systems, various forms of the family exist.

The entire statement was actually designed to make same-sex marriage legitimate and same-sex couples supported, without having to mention that goal. Our first proposal was simply to insert the word *traditional* before the word *forms*, a small change, but a large limitation. Even that one-word addition would have been distasteful to the original drafters, but we proposed a further statement that caused quite a stir. We proposed, in addition, a comma in place of the period after the word *exist*, followed by a very specific qualifier:

In different cultural, political, and social systems, various traditional forms of the family exist, recognizing that a sustainable family is a family of father, mother, and children, whose loving nurturing and self-reliant qualities extend through the generations.

Our suggested change to this paragraph was bold and it was met with hostility.

To actually propose including a definition of family as requiring a mother and a father was a frontal assault on the Women's Caucus and their coalition. One woman from that group was so angry that she yelled at Richard, "Men like you don't deserve to live!" Some of his cohorts from United Families were fearful that it might be a death threat, but Richard was not. He had received death threats before and he knew what they felt like.

Another woman who opposed the traditional definition of family shook her head at Richard in dismay and said: "You're insane. There hasn't been a definition of family as a mother and a father since 1949!" Clearly intending to damn his definition as archaic, the woman's statement instead fascinated Richard. 1949. So there had once been such a definition in UN documents. It was a precedent he could use. He sent Bradley Roylance in search of the 1949 record. It seemed a daunting task. There were volumes of documents, but the most amazing thing happened. The first volume that Bradley picked up fell open to the page where the definition was found.

The next two days passed in a whirlwind of intensity: writing recommendations to substitute for bracketed material, and suggested amendments to other components, then spreading the word among the huge coalition that had now emerged to fight the Western nations.

Wednesday night late, a large group went out to eat dinner. None of them had eaten all day. They were a little afraid to leave the compound but decided there was safety in numbers, and they found a little restaurant not far away. The place sold Turkish food but not, it appeared, to Turks. Only tourists were seated there. Richard ate little. The adrenaline wouldn't stop pumping—even for a dinner break. He went back to the Hilton and called Melany. That was probably the nourishment he needed. He had called her earlier in the day as well. As he stood at the telephone Richard noticed, for the first time, that he was being followed. His unwelcome shadow was trying to listen to everything he said. He found himself whispering, and Melany said she couldn't hear him. He tried to explain that they were being overheard and he ended up cutting his conversation short.

Wednesday night it was easy to stay awake. Richard couldn't have slept if he had tried. Committee Two had been convened and would remain in session all night. Normally a drafting committee would adjourn in the evenings, but the two chairmen, sympathetic to those fighting for the traditional family language, opted not to adjourn the meeting until consensus was achieved—no matter how long it took. It was a brilliant move. If the committee had adjourned, small private meetings would have taken place in which members could find ways to manipulate the process. This way, everything had to be done under the glare of very public lights. Richard had learned that there is little to fear from what happens in public. So keeping the meeting in session was important—although heavy in the wear-and-tear department.

Once, Thursday, Richard went back to the hotel to shower and change clothes. Someone joked about the advantage of his beard because some of the others had begun to look unshaven. Late Thursday he lay down in the hallway of the Hilton and put his head on his thin plastic briefcase to catch a thirty-minute nap. As his eyes were closing, Richard thought of the absurdity of his lying on the marble floor of the Istanbul Hilton with his head on a plastic briefcase, and feeling as if it were a feather bed, with down pillows—as if he were being serenaded by celestial choirs—so badly did he need to just recline.

But thirty minutes later, when he awoke, he had muscle aches he hadn't had before. There was no real rest and no real food for the seventy-two hours it took to break down the resistance of the Western nations.

Richard continued to be followed everywhere he went. Several women took turns doing it. They were obvious and annoying—and especially troublesome when he went to the phones, which he did every few hours. Usually it was to call Melany. Her strength nurtured him and kept him going. Once it was to call the MasterCard people again, because he kept writing and copying, writing and copying. Delegates kept asking for large numbers of copies. By now he knew the woman at the bank by her first name, and this time he asked for a much bigger increase in his limit.

Sometimes the delegates who asked for copies would come to the United Families people with their badges turned away from view. Richard came to understand that these turned-badge delegates were often from the opposition and were trying to deplete and destroy the copies he had made at such dear personal expense. Richard put out the instruction that if a badge was turned, the delegate was to be questioned as to whom he or she represented—not that they would withhold copies from any group that was willing to be identified, only that if they refused to be identified they were refused the copies.

Rumors are always rampant in a microcosm like the UN compound. At the Hilton Hotel that week, many of the rumors were about Richard. Some of them were quite amusing to him when they reached his ears. One was that he was a spy for Jesse Helms and that he was at the phones whispering to Helms several times a day. Many thought that he was representing a well-funded, well-oiled organization, and everyone wondered what it was. Once the woman who followed him badgered him to tell her where all his money was coming from. "There's obviously a lot of money and a lot of power behind you! Who is it? Who's financing this monstrous campaign?" Richard assured her that he was, in fact, sponsoring himself with an overdrawn MasterCard, that he had credentials from an International Studies Center which had paid only for an economy airline ticket and a six-dollar-a-day shared hotel room. Richard did not convince the woman. She sneered and called him a liar.

Once Richard overheard two delegates talking. One was a Pakistani fellow he recognized. They were complaining that the conference was topsy-turvy and that consensus was going to be difficult. Then one of them cocked his head and jokingly said: "Hi, I'm from the Mormons!" The other feigned horror and said mockingly, "Oh NO!" as he issued a little shrill scream. Richard, observing from a safe distance, watched them laugh at his expense. Strangely, he thought the joke a compliment he had not earned alone, and wanted only to share the credit with the Catholics and the Muslims, and with all the groups who were working so hard. But he said nothing and turned to walk in the other direction without being noticed.

Much of what we did during those three days and three nights was to give support to those who had issued pro-family statements but were being besieged by those who wanted to have the brackets removed. The Women's Caucus resurrected an old theme from the Beijing Conference: "Take the Brackets off Women's Lives!" They felt personally attacked by our stance and they fought defensively, with condescension instead of debate. It was increasingly difficult to stand up to them. The Catholic group was strong. They had fought relatively alone at the Cairo Conference and they were, by now, well organized. Some feared, however, that the Islamic group might not hold up under the pressure. Indeed, their pressure was great because they were widely (although wrongly) persecuted as being a society that was barbarous toward women. Nevertheless, the coalition needn't have worried. The Islamic Conference held fast.

Perhaps all of the groups were experiencing the same fear that their allies would not be able to hold against the onslaught of derision. At one point a group of Muslims asked Richard: "Why do you do this? What is in it for you? Is this based on your political belief, or is this based on faith?" Richard responded quickly. The answer was easy. "Both," he said. "I think it is best from a political perspective because history tells us and shows us that societies that recognize religious rights and parental rights, that work to retain the values that religion teaches—clearly those societies create more stable regimes.

"But ultimately," he said, "I'm doing it because I believe it is what my God wants me to do."

There were smiles all around, and Richard realized that he had passed a sort of test. Prior to that moment the Islamic Conference was pleased for the help Richard had given—especially coming as it did from a citizen of a Western nation—but they had not yet begun to really trust him. That day, that answer to their question, was the beginning of a faithful friendship between Richard and the Islamic delegates.

As Friday afternoon progressed, Richard began to be truly exhausted. Adrenaline, evidently, couldn't last forever. For the first time, he was hungry. He had been given something that worked like scrip, with which he could buy food. Meals were served at normal mealtimes, but he was always occupied then.

The money substitute, however, would also work in vending machines. He decided that ice cream would be cool and pleasant going down. But when the machine dislodged the ice cream it was no longer frozen. Moreover, it was ejected smartly, and the sticky thick white liquid spurted all over Richard's shoes. Perhaps a sandwich would be best after all. But when the sandwich came out the bread was wet and rotted; the salami looked green and dangerous. Richard discarded the meat and the scooped-out center of the gooey bread. He ate the crusts and hoped for the best. After his experience with the vending machines, his appetite was pretty well dissipated anyway.

The conference had been scheduled to close on Friday afternoon, and most of his United Families friends had made airline reservations that depended on that schedule. By sunset most of Richard's NGO friends had left, but the meetings of Committee Two continued. Johnson Mwara came around to say good-bye. He gave Richard a big hug and told him that he felt that the elders of Israel had made a great impact on this conference.

A big parade had been scheduled for 5:00 P.M. Friday to celebrate the completion of the Habitat II Agenda. But at 5:00 there was still nothing to celebrate. The decision was made to have the parade anyway. After the sun set, fireworks were scheduled. There was still nothing to celebrate, but the fireworks, too, were presented as scheduled.

I walked out on the square, where there were flags and flower gardens. The UN compound was up on a hill and afforded a beautiful view of Istanbul. My friends had left, but I was not alone in the square. We all watched the fireworks, fully aware that the arguing and unpleasantness were still going on in the meeting of Committee Two. I couldn't help but smile when the man next to me suggested that the *real* fireworks were going on inside the Hilton.

✿

Although Richard was going to remain in Istanbul for what he planned to be a couple of days of sightseeing, he decided to check out of the Ulubat Hotel. He craved western-style plumbing and a bed with a real mattress. After the fireworks he boarded the UN shuttle to go pack up and check out of the Ulubat.

When he arrived at the hotel he opened the door of his room and came face-to-face with the small mirror that was hanging on the wall. The man in the mirror unnerved him. He thought the man looked old—perhaps eighty or maybe older. He was thin-looking and drawn. It almost frightened him. He diverted his startled stare and looked around the room.

For a moment he was almost nostalgic. He even sniffed the air and thought of Susan's aromatic transformer—the odor that had wafted down the hall and been his bedtime fragrance so many nights these past two weeks while the indefatigable Susan had worked into the nighttime. Now the transformer was surely packed up in one of the K Mart plastic storage boxes—as were the computer and the laser printer.

Suddenly and inexorably, Richard was drawn to the plywood platform. For ninety minutes he was hearing those celestial choirs again. The nap had not been planned. When he awoke he looked at his watch and jolted to his feet. It took him only a few minutes to pack his bags, and then he took a cab to the local Best Western hotel, checked in, left his luggage, and took the waiting cab back to the Hilton.

When he got back to the conference it was midnight. In the meeting room of Committee Two the United States and the other Western nations were still holding to their insistence that the brackets be removed without substitute or additional language. But the determination of the opposition was at least equally strong. The Islamic Conference was holding, and the Catholics were holding, and the G-77 nations were holding, and so were the Pacific Rim States, and China. Intimidation wasn't working.

And so, a few hours later, in the embryonic hours of Saturday, June 15, 1996, the great nations of the western world capitulated. Consensus was declared. The family was defined as including a father and a mother, with the language of the 1949 document that Brad Roylance had found. Family and parental rights were listed alongside the rights of the child. Reproductive health rights were limited by the law of sovereign nations and by cultural and religious tradition. What some of the people there had called "a new wave of imperialism, this time *cultural* imperialism," had been turned back.

The delegates from Committee Two finally adjourned their informal session and took their places for a grand ceremony by the flags and the flowers, just as had been planned to happen in the afternoon before the parade. The speeches were grandiose, self-serving, and "colorful." But they largely ignored the magnitude of what had happened that night.

Later, Richard would join others in hailing the Habitat II Agenda as "The Istanbul Miracle." But that Saturday dawn he was only tired and numb. He took a cab to the Best Western and sank into what felt like a coma.

CHAPTER 9

Alone in Istanbul

Fourteen hours later Richard turned over in bed and blinked his eyes open. After he realized that he was still in Istanbul, he stretched out his full length and luxuriated in the soft mattress and the clean sheets. Ah, it felt great! A few more blinks and he was ready to try to focus on his wristwatch. It was six o'clock. He concluded that it must be P.M. That made the most sense.

Once his actual whereabouts in time and space were established, he thought about the rug shop in the corner of the square at the Hagia Sofia. That Monday night (could it be only two weeks ago?) when Richard had bought the large rugs, he had seen a runner that he argued with himself about buying. During the past difficult days he sometimes kept himself sane by dreaming about that runner. So as soon as he had showered and dressed, he headed toward the Hagia Sofia and the eager merchant.

The man with the big belt buckle was ever so happy to see Richard again. And yes, the runner was still there. Was there anything else he could help him with? Could he show him some beautiful silver? Richard answered that no, he had quite enough, and then he remembered that he had no souvenirs for the family. "Oh, maybe something for the children." He spied some lavishly embroidered hats and vests over to one side. They would be perfect. His shopping was complete.

As he walked out onto the square, Richard remembered that he was hungry. He had eaten his last meal three days ago—and not a full meal at that. He looked for a restaurant. This time he wanted to be sure that he found one where the locals ate. He was, after all, in a land he had never experienced before.

He found a crowded place and went inside. Lined up behind a glass were rows of magnificent looking casseroles—vegetables and meat that looked so tender and moist they must have been marinated. He walked down the buffet line and chose several. He was getting hungrier with every step. At the end of the line a server stacked multiple pieces of a kind of pita bread on top of all his main dishes, and the tray he took to the cashier looked like it could have come out of a cornucopia.

Richard sat down with great anticipation. People were staring at the size of his dinner, but he told himself that they didn't understand. They didn't know he hadn't eaten for three days. He took a bite. It was wonderful! Another bite. Delicious! He tried scooping up the meat and vegetables with his bread as he saw the others doing. He was a little awkward with it, but— well, he was in Turkey, wasn't he? He tried it again. Then he stopped. He couldn't go any further. He was feeling uncomfortably full, and almost sick to his stomach. He tried another bite, but had to put the dripping bread back on his plate. The three days without eating had left him able to eat *less* food, not more. He was embarrassed to leave his plate almost completely full of all those magnificent dishes that had captured his fancy, but that was what he had to do. He could feel that he would be ill if he continued to eat.

For a while he walked around and loved the leisurely pace

with which he was able to enjoy the sights and sounds of Istanbul. He didn't run into United Nations badges anywhere. Those delegates and NGO people who hadn't left Friday night had left this morning, he supposed. He luxuriated in the role of a tourist. It never occurred to him that he was alone and probably should have been frightened. The blood in the street seemed like so long ago.

Richard still wanted very much to see the Suleymaniye Mosque. But he had trouble communicating that to the people he asked—or maybe they just had trouble with the answer. Perhaps he would have to go home and simply reread that *National Geographic.*

There was one more thing on his list. He wanted to try a Turkish bath. One in particular. Caligula had used one that he had heard about—and he understood that it had been in continuous operation since that time with no changes in the process. What a way to experience the indulgence of the Roman era! He went in and paid what seemed like an enormous price of $14. He told them he wanted the full treatment.

Richard shed his clothing and wrapped himself in the large towel that was provided. They showed him into a room where there was a massive and well-worn slab of marble. He took his place on the huge wheel as if he were a piece of pie. He lay there for a while while water was poured on hot stones to make steam. The wet heat was soothing. "Ah," he thought, "this is a far cry from the marble floors of the Hilton." After a time, he felt his muscles begin to return to a position where they had not been for some time. Finally, the attendant came in and asked if Richard would like to have the optional cold water bath, and when, with a spirit of adventure, he said yes, the attendant poured buckets of icy water over him that startled his system.

The next step was to be slapped all over with a bundle of sticks tied together like a broom. It brought all of his blood to the surface and replaced the chill with the warm feeling of a brisk massage. By that time the relaxation was so profound that it was difficult to stand up again. Once he did stand, moreover, he wanted nothing else except his clean-sheeted bed.

Back at the Best Western, he called Melany. She asked him how he was doing and he answered from the trance of his total relaxation that he was doing wonderfully! "Melany," he said, "if we could have Turkish baths in the United States it would completely remove the need for valium. Not a good thing for the pharmaceutical economy, I know, but glorious for humankind."

Richard had scarcely thought about the United Nations for this entire evening. He'd had a restful nightfall, all alone in Istanbul, with a real bed to come back to, and a real bathroom to brush his teeth in. It was not late but he fell asleep again, still feeling the tingle of the broomful of sticks.

CHAPTER 10

My Friends, My Brethren

Sunday again. Richard lay in bed and delighted in the Sabbath feeling. "Six days shalt thou labor and do all thy work," the commandment said. Actually, he mused, it was thirteen days he had labored—thirteen long days—but he had *done all his work*. Rarely had he had such a sense of having done the work he was sent to do. This was how every Sunday should feel, he supposed. If only it could always be so.

As he lay there Richard thought about his friends the Friedmans. Some years earlier they had attended a religious camp where the routine was a week of strenuous physical labor. It was work they weren't used to, and it required every bit of their being to stay with it. At the end of the week, when they began their Jewish *shabat*, it was with sore muscles and with an enormous sense of accomplishment. "Never before," he remembered their reporting, "has Friday night been so meaningful for us. When we lighted our candles we entered into our day of rest without ambivalence and without equivocation. We were so exhausted and so grateful. It was like a celebration of the Lord's allowing us our accomplishment. It was a defining moment of *shabat* for us."

Richard remembered thinking it romantic when the Friedmans told their story. Now that he was experiencing it for himself he understood that it was more profound than that.

He lifted himself from his "real" mattress and went into his "real" and private bathroom to ready himself for church. When he left the hotel the sunshine felt extraordinarily pleasant.

The previous Sunday he had been part of a large and congenial group that had accompanied Elder and Sister Didier to church. Today Richard was alone. Last Sunday seemed like forever ago. Still, he had no trouble in finding the place a second time. He looked forward to seeing Jonathan's parents again. The spirit of their service began to descend on him before he even arrived at their apartment.

Elder and Sister Lofgren were the only missionaries in Turkey. They were not allowed to proselyte—only to answer questions that others might ask about the Church. The little plaque on the building where they lived announced that it was the location of The Church of Jesus Christ of Latter-day Saints, and often that did indeed invite questions. Even when the questions came, however, it was difficult. Most Church materials had not been translated into Turkish, and like missionaries of old they taught only from the scriptures. Their faith overwhelmed and humbled me.

Richard climbed the stairs to the Lofgrens' apartment and entered the makeshift chapel. There were so few gathered there. The previous week the ranks had been swollen with the United Families people, while today he was one of only two or three handfuls of participants. The branch president was a Turkish businessman who was there with his family, as he had been the week before. He spoke fluent English and kindly did so from the pulpit for Richard's benefit. The warm spirit of the meeting comforted Richard.

After church he stood for a few minutes and looked out the broad picture window. He was struck with the view. They were high on a hill and below lay Istanbul, the city that would forever represent a kind of nativity to him. It was not that, at that point, he understood the experience exactly, but he did feel its portent. He looked out at the Bosphorus. It was the picturesque body of water that separated Europe from Asia, but Richard, that early afternoon, focused more on the majestic bridge that spanned the channel and connected the two. He could see the Golden Horn Waterway and the Blue Mosque, and Hagia Sophia where he had bought the rugs on that first day and again last night. On the other side there was another large mosque. He asked the Lofgrens what it was and they said, "That's the Suleymaniye Mosque." Richard knew at once how he would spend the afternoon. He thanked the Lofgrens for their kind dinner invitation but declined it.

It was not easy to find a taxi but Richard managed it. When he told the driver his destination, however, the driver said that he would not be able to take him the whole of the distance. "The roads are narrow and not large enough for me to go there. I will take you to the bottom of the hill and you can walk up." Walking up hill did not appeal to Richard. He was still exhausted from his harrowing fortnight. But this was significant to him. "Okay, drop me off as close as you can come."

He pulled out the large awkward map he had purchased two weeks before and tried again to locate the Suleymaniye Mosque. The taxi driver spoke up: "You might as well put your map away. Most of the streets aren't on the map. I'll point you in the right direction. Just keep climbing up, and you'll find it. No problem." And he pulled his cab up to the bottom of the hill. Richard paid him and, with a sigh, started his ascent.

✳

It was a long walk up the hill. And not a straight one. Sometimes I thought I had made the wrong turn and got lost. But just as that seemed sure, I would see a minaret of the mosque and know that I was headed in the right direction. It seemed so confusing because sometimes I would see a minaret on my right hand, and sometimes on my left. I kept remembering that the cab driver had said to "just keep climbing up, and you'll find it. No problem." So I stayed the course. At each turn I took the uphill road.

✳

Often the old stone buildings obscured the view entirely. Most of the streets were so narrow that Richard could have spread his arms and touched both sides at once.

Richard was suddenly tired. He had, after all, lost twenty-eight pounds in two weeks. His weakened body was ill equipped for such a strenuous walk. A little rest, perhaps, and then he could go on. There was nowhere to sit, so he leaned against a wall and caught his breath. The street was so narrow that he had to move around the corner because some others wanted to pass. He turned, and there it was! Looming large in front of him was the Suleymaniye Mosque. No warning. Just: there it was. The abrupt discovery almost startled him.

Outside the mosque were men who offered their services as guides. Richard hired one of them and was escorted inside. They removed their shoes and entered in their stocking feet. The odor of stocking feet by the hundreds reached Richard's nostrils, and he recoiled a bit. Great numbers of people were there, the men on one side and the women on the other—more women than men. The guide took Richard to a fenced-off area for nonbelievers, where he could see the magnificent mosaics and the overall splendor of the architecture.

The whole of the place was lit by candles—dozens of them; no, maybe hundreds. Huge wrought-iron, wheel-like candelabras hung very low from the high ceiling; so low that he thought if he reached up he might be able to touch them. On this sunny afternoon the candlelight competed with light streaming in the windowpanes. The windows were highlighted with pieces of colored glass. Not that they were stained glass windows in the European cathedral sense, but they were exquisite and caught the sun in dazzling ways.

As his guide pointed out the different features of the building and identified them with tenets of the Muslim faith, Richard's eye happened to look downward, and he caught sight of the carpet. It was stunning. Every three feet or so it repeated a pattern that was about eighteen inches wide. In that large mosque it seemed as if there were acres and acres of the hand-tied, magnificent work of art. He was overwhelmed with the thought of the labor, of the skill and the artistry he was seeing. He had been, after all, enthralled with Turkish rugs, and here he was seeing the quintessential example. At first that was all he saw. His intense interest in the art form, however, led him to look further.

I noticed some sort of plant or tree in the pattern. My guide had already explained to me that, honoring the second commandment, Muslims did not make works of art that depicted creatures of any kind. My first thought, upon noticing the plant, was to mention to my guide that it seemed the prohibition did not extend to all life forms. I looked closer. The plant was a tree. At the bottom of the pattern the tree was in bud, in the middle it was in bloom, and at the top it was laden with fruit. White fruit. Above the tree at the very top of each pattern was a chandelier.

The guide explained that when a Muslim knelt to pray he leaned forward and put his hands at the sides of the fruited tree and placed his forehead on the light of Allah that was symbolized by the chandelier. The guide called my attention to the fact that the fruit of the tree was pure and white. He told me that when a man focuses on the light that Allah sends to him, he reaches eternal life, where he will live with Allah and partake of the pure white fruit. "It is the tree of life," he said.

Looking across the little fence that separated us I saw hundreds of Muslims praying on the tree of life. They were expecting to be in the presence of their God and eat of the fruit of the tree of life just as I was expecting to be in the presence of my God and eat of the fruit of the tree of life. The identification was overwhelming. All at once it was clear that we were all striving to be ultimately in the presence of the same God. It sounds obvious I know, but to me, that day, it was suddenly real.

Richard stood new-begotten. He was changed in a fundamental way. He was at once totally insignificant and sublimely important.

Somewhere in the far reaches of his senses he could hear the guide still talking, but it didn't matter any more. Nothing mattered except the hundreds of worshippers on the other side of the barrier. His heart welled up with love for them. The feeling was so tender that he cried. Spirit to spirit they were his family. They were the children of Abraham, and so was he. They took hope and direction from the symbol of the tree of life, and so did he. God had kept His promise to Abraham that Ishmael would be blessed. Hagar's son had indeed been made into a great nation (see Genesis 21:18).

The people from the Islamic Conference had become Richard's friends at the Habitat II meetings, and now, now—in his very core—from this moment on they would be brethren to him.

Richard's heart was filled with love: "My friends, my brethren. You heard me because I brought you the voice of the prophet of the God of Abraham. You don't know that Gordon B. Hinckley is the prophet of your God, but you heard his voice. And you, my brothers, had the courage to stand up for truth that you recognized and resonated to—a courage I found within myself only by painful effort, in spite of my good fortune to know the identity of that prophet."

Richard's mind raced. Everyone. Everyone. He loved them all because he knew now for certain that God did. The Spirit had given him the most profound of witnesses. His heart went out even to his adversaries at Habitat II—the better world he was fighting for was for them too. And the better world—the best life that mortality could offer—was described in a proclamation to the world, sent forth by prophets of the true and living God. Richard's work in support of that proclamation would never again be a matter of contention for him. All the rancor and bitterness from insults and threats—they were all washed out of him and he was clean.

So many things were manifested together. Complex concepts suddenly were clear to Richard—simple things became all-important: God existed and Richard was connected to Him. He knew Him.

✵

Whereas I had believed myself involved in an angry battle against evil people, I now—in one instant and powerful change of disposition—wanted only to touch their hearts. I wanted them to understand that unborn children are our brothers and

sisters, and if I used to want to regulate abortion because I thought it was "bad," now it was because I loved those children. I knew that those who saw me as their enemy were concerned about the women—and I was moved by that, but I wanted them to know that I loved both the children *and* the mothers.

I remembered what President Hinckley had said about those "burdened with same-sex attraction," and I grieved at how heavy that burden must be. At the same time I understood that as caring as it was to want gratification for those so burdened, it was not what was in their best interest. God had something more, something better than that for them.

It all came down to comprehending something as basic and obvious as life. I saw that it was all about life giving, life sustaining, and life nurturing. It is the only part of Godhood that we can begin to understand here, and if one is not engaged in it one's entire life loses its most important aspect of meaning. I wanted all those people who were fighting on the other side to have that meaning.

I wanted the perspective of eternal life and eternal love for everyone, and I was willing to commit to whatever was necessary to give them that opportunity.

The full measure of it all made Richard long for home. He ached to be with Melany and the children. If his reservations had allowed it, he would have been on an airplane within the hour. Instead he went back to the Best Western and telephoned them. He knew that Melany could tell on the phone that something important had happened, but efforts at explaining it were inadequate. He could only tell her that he loved her. Oh, how he loved her!

CHAPTER 11

Homeward

Richard's last stop in Istanbul was, like his first, at a rug shop. This time, however, for a prayer rug. He asked not a single question about its workmanship, the number of knots or the quality of its ties. His only concern was that it be an exact replica of the carpet in the Suleymaniye Mosque. This time there was no one with him to evaluate the colors. Being color blind is seldom a significant handicap, but he wished now he could be sure his prayer rug was a perfect and exact copy. He had to trust the merchant that it was.

Packed up and ready, he waited in the lobby of the Best Western hotel for a bus to take him to the airport. There was a mirror there and he glanced into it. The man in the mirror still had the weathered aspect he had had at the Ulubat two days before. Richard looked and felt old.

He was pensive getting on the airplane—and glad he had packed his scriptures in his carry-on. The plane was still on the tarmac when he got his scriptures out, but he didn't open them right away. Instead he looked out the window. Exactly two weeks ago he had arrived here. He had flown into the sun and missed the night. He smiled when he realized that he had actually been tired ever since. For today's trip the sun would be at his back. Quite a different vision.

Two weeks before, coming from New York, Richard had been frightened—and actually with more cause than he then knew. But if, at that point, Jonah was his soul mate, well, Captain Moroni was his hero. Richard did have scriptural heroes sometimes. His sense of theater lent itself to the fantasy of playing a role. As Captain Moroni, his fantasy battle was against people who wanted to be king and were ripe in iniquity. His was an angry war, and he fought it under a banner of his own rent clothing: "In memory of our God, our religion, and freedom, and our peace, our wives, and our children" (Alma 46:12). As he thought of it now, he could visualize the title of liberty fastened to a pole and being carried into the heat of the *real* battle of Committee Two. He shook his head and smiled.

His fantasy was changed now. Today his hero was Alma. He opened his Book of Mormon to Alma chapter 4 and read verse 15: "And now it came to pass that Alma, having seen the afflictions of the humble followers of God, and the persecutions which were heaped upon them by the remainder of his people, and seeing all their inequality, began to be very sorrowful; nevertheless the Spirit of the Lord did not fail him."

He kept reading through the verses where Alma chose to give up the judgment seat in order "that he might pull down, by the word of God, all the pride and craftiness and all the contentions which were among his people, seeing no way that he might reclaim them save it were in bearing down in pure testimony" (Alma 4:19).

He noticed that in his mind the word was *chose*. Alma chose. In the process there was a huge sacrifice to make, but he chose.

Richard and Melany had often had conversations about "choosing." Richard always said that he did his duty because he felt he must—that in his view he had no choice. Melany always said that of course it was a choice, and that when he didn't acknowledge that he took the nobility out of what he did.

Well, Melany's right and I'm right. We choose, of course, but it's more like we make one grand choice and then after that we simply follow where that leads us, and we have no more choice because we've yielded it already. That first grand choice is between comfort and growth; because the choice for growth means that we must make subsequent choices that make us uncomfortable.

Maybe the reason some of us believe that we have no choice is simply that we lack the courage to let ourselves make those difficult decisions as we go along. Comfort is hard to sacrifice, and when each choice is considered on an individual basis the comfort will always beckon. So—well, call it lack of courage if you like, but for me, I say: there is no choice. The commitment to growth has been made.

After this leg of the flight, Richard would change planes and there would be another leg: back home to Utah. But the journey would not be over. Soon he would have to do his humble equivalent of giving up his judgment seat in order to (uncomfortably) bear down in pure testimony as to the truth of the Proclamation on the Family.

Only he didn't know that then.

He snapped the cover on his Book of Mormon and closed his eyes. He thanked his Father in Heaven again for what had happened in the Suleymaniye Mosque—for the infusion of spiritual strength that he had received, even as his body was at its weakest. For the understanding of so many things, and for the love—for His very presence.

Richard's heart almost burst when he got off the airplane in Salt Lake City and saw his family. He was able to keep his composure, though, until four-year-old Rex put his face against his and clung to him with such trusting tiny arms.

EPILOGUE

Melany noticed a difference in Richard right away. He was softened. He was happier. And so was she.

As soon as Richard got home they had to move out of their house and begin building the house on the hill. Meanwhile they moved into the dressing rooms at the Orem Hale Center Theater (at the kind invitation of their friends Cody and Linda Hale and Cody and Anne Swenson). Life was somewhat discombobulated for that year. It was difficult, because Richard's excitement with the big house had begun to pale. In addition, he was trying to put the whole Istanbul episode into perspective: it had been such a profound experience. Clearly it required something of him. But what? He was continually haunted by the question "Where have you been?" that the Saudi Arabian ambassador had asked him that morning after his four-minute speech. He found himself repeating the question to the dean of the law school: "Where have we been?" And he smiled after he heard himself saying essentially what Susan had said to him: "We need to DO something."

The months passed. When spring came he received a mailing telling him about an upcoming United Nations conference in Nairobi, Kenya. It included a listing of individuals already scheduled to participate in the NGO Forum there. The

Women's Caucus was represented in exceptional numbers. Richard began calling the United Families people and some of the friends he had made in Istanbul. "Are you going to Nairobi?" he asked. Most of the responses were that no, they weren't going this time. There was a general feeling that the triumph in Istanbul had taken care of things.

Nevertheless, Richard had a nagging uneasiness about the force of numbers planning to attend from the Women's Caucus. He decided to go to Nairobi. He took with him a couple of bright law students and a faculty member from the Kennedy Center for International Studies.

In Nairobi, Richard found that the committed social engineers had decided to largely ignore Istanbul. They quoted the Cairo Conference, the Beijing Conference, but never Habitat II. Something had gone awry in Istanbul. They didn't understand why, but the coronation of all their plans had not taken place. Better, then, to try once again to build on the Beijing foundation and simply disregard the snag they had inexplicably met at Habitat II.

Apparently it was not going to be possible for the group in defense of families to simply rely on their achievements in the Habitat Agenda. The price of liberty, it seems, really *is* eternal vigilance.

The tiny group from BYU experienced unthinkable obstacles in Nairobi, including the contracting of a deadly virus by one of the law students. But not only was there a miraculous healing, once again there were miracles in the results of the conference.

Nairobi was an impetus. When Richard returned home he began to be able to put his thoughts in order regarding the role that BYU should take in bringing together the forces that wanted to fight for the traditional family. One of his research assistants, a computer-savvy young law student, suggested a

Web site. Notwithstanding the fact that many of the developing nations that were part of the coalition did not have access to computers, the Web site seemed a good way to begin. Richard named the site NGO Family Voice. There was so much talk of the need for a variety of "voices" that a place of advocacy for the family seemed rightfully identified as one of those "voices."

But there was need for more than just a Web site. Coordinating efforts for future UN meetings, strengthening resolve between meetings, writing papers informing the general public—all of these things and more were necessary. Richard presented a plan—first to his dean, then to the director of the Kennedy Center, and then to the president of the University. An executive director and a secretary were funded for a trial period of two years. Kay Balmforth, a mother of six grown children, an attorney, and a former student of Richard's, was hired as executive director. She brought with her an extensive experience in litigation regarding family matters and proved a great resource in some of the midnight writing that was still going on at the UN conferences. And the UN conferences seemed to follow one another in rapid succession. Richard was off to New York, off to Geneva, off to Rome. Now, however, not only did law students travel along but also Kay was there—another pair of eyes to catch the legal pitfalls in the parsed language, another source of expertise to sidestep them. Richard felt the lessening of the burden.

In Rome in 1998 a conference met to establish an international criminal court. The powers sought for the court were so far-reaching that this time even the United States spoke out against it. But it was the logical next step, considering the previous UN documents. It was too late now for this great Western nation to start worrying about national sovereignty in such matters, having previously yielded so much as the price of calling the dance for the rest of the world. It was sad that Rome resulted in a major defeat for those trying to keep the United Nations from indulging in what is necessarily undemocratic government. For the traditional family, however, some success was achieved. A major effort was launched by the opposition to label it a war crime for a country to deny abortion on demand, or to "discriminate" against same-sex marriage. That effort was effectively turned back—or at least, Richard felt, staved off for this generation.

It was interesting that much of the struggle in Rome was over the selection criteria for the panel of International Criminal Court judges. Typical of their long-range view, the Women's Caucus gave their greatest push to including in the documents a requirement that all judges have experience demonstrating sympathy for Caucus causes.

The meeting in Rome lasted for five exhausting weeks. Richard and Melany had spent so little time together lately that he planned a romantic getaway for the two of them to Sorrento at the end of the meeting. Richard had been a missionary in Italy as a young man, and the dream of bringing Melany there was particularly heartfelt. When Melany arrived in Rome, however, the conference was still going full-bore. Melany pitched in and helped with the endless enterprise. They never got to Sorrento.

In all ways NGO Family Voice had become a demanding mistress for Richard. There was very little time for the consulting that always kept his income flowing. The new house soon sported a "for sale" sign. But it mattered less, anyway. Richard's mind and heart were spent on things that made the luxury of it all quite unimportant. Besides, the house included separate quarters for Richard's parents, and just as it was being prepared for occupancy Richard's mother passed away.

Over the course of the years following Istanbul, Richard's friendship with leaders of the world religions and with family oriented people from every corner of the globe had become a comfort and an inspiration to him. When NGO Family Voice sponsored a World Family Policy Forum at BYU in January of 1999, the support was overwhelming. Religious and government leaders came from the north and the south, the east and the west—for one and all an important sharing of ideas and a unique bonding in brotherhood.

When the Forum was over, Richard started letting his beard grow again. He and Melany (and their whole family except for Brinton, who was still on his mission) went into rehearsal for another production of *Fiddler on the Roof*. If they missed celebrating the twenty-fifth anniversary of their playing that role for the first time, they at least could celebrate their twenty-fifth *wedding* anniversary singing that important song to one another.

In the first week of June, 1999, the two-year trial period was declared a success and NGO Family Voice, now more broadly named as The World Family Policy Center, became a permanent reality at BYU. Support for its mission has continued to flow in from high and unlikely places.

It hasn't stopped being difficult for Richard. He still encounters some bitter opposition. And the time away from his family is hard for a man whose wife and children mean everything to him. He is, however, sustained by his family—and not only his immediate family. The replica of the prayer rug from the Suleymaniye Mosque sits atop his piano. He sees it every day—and every time he does, he is reminded of the brotherhood that now motivates him. Sometimes that rare fulness of the heart with which he was blessed on that Sabbath afternoon returns. When it does, it overwhelms him with reverence.

NOTES

1. "PrepCom" is UNSpeak for meetings designed to prepare drafts of documents to be adopted as policy by upcoming UN conferences. Language that achieves "consensus" at the PrepComs is generally expected to be adopted by consensus at the conference itself and become "policy," "customary norm."

2. Joseph Stein, *Fiddler on the Roof*, in *Best American Plays, 6th Series, 1963–67*, John Gassner and Chize Barnes, eds. (New York: Crown Publishers, Inc., 1987), p. 402.

3. The full text of Professor Wilkins' address is included as Appendix A.

4. Alva Myrdal, *Nation and Family* (Cambridge: M.I.T. Press, March 1968), pp. 115, 116.

5. Myrdal, op. cit., p. 128.

6. Sissela Bok, *Alva Myrdal, a Daughter's Memoir* (Reading, Ma.: Addison-Wesley Publishing Co., Inc., 1991), p. 30.

7. Jan Myrdal, *Twelve Going on Thirteen* (Chicago: Ravenswood Books, 1995), p. 12.

8. Myrdal, op. cit., p. 124.

9. The full text of the Arab statement is included as Appendix C.

10. The full text of the UK statement is included as Appendix D.

11. Statement distributed by Bella Abzug at a PrepCom for the Beijing conference 3 April 1995, a copy of which is in the possession of the authors.

The Impact of UN Conference Declarations on International and Domestic Law

Richard G. Wilkins
and
Bradley N. Roylance

Delivered by Richard G. Wilkins at the NGO (Non-Governmental Organization)
Forum of the Second United Nations Conference
on Human Settlements (Habitat II)
Instanbul, Turkey, 4 June 1996

The United Nations General Assembly periodically convenes world conferences on issues of global concern. The most recent conferences (e.g., the Cairo Conference on Population and Development, the Fourth World Conference on Women held in Beijing, and the Rio Environmental Conference), building upon work done in earlier UN meetings, have received significant worldwide attention and have been perceived as influential norm-setting events.[1] The Istanbul Conference on Human Settlements, Habitat II, also builds upon an earlier conference, the 1976 UN Conference on Human Settlements held in Vancouver, B.C., Canada. Habitat II, like the earlier conferences, will engender exhaustive debate and produce a signed declaration setting forth plans of action to implement worldwide goals established during the conference. Establishing goals and even subscribing to them, however, is quite different from implementing those precepts. The question remains, therefore, whether the Habitat II declaration will have any real impact on either international or domestic law.

This Article explores the impact of UN conferences, not only upon international law, but upon the domestic law of conference participants. Part I discusses the historical international law framework within which UN conferences operate. Part II then briefly looks at the international law context of UN conferences and the declarations that emerge from them. Part III, finally, looks more closely at the specific formal and informal means by which conference declarations may have an appreciable impact upon the internal policy of participating nations.

This brief analysis suggests that UN conference documents, although not technically binding upon participating nations, nevertheless are an important influence in shaping and solidifying the normative concepts of international law. The conference documents, moreover, may have significant impact upon the domestic policy of signatory nations even without formal enforcement mechanisms. Great care, therefore, is warranted in crafting the precise language incorporated into a formal conference declaration.

I. The Historical and Modern Roots of International Law

"[C]ontemporary international organizations cannot be fully understood without some reference to their philosophical and historical background."[2] We therefore review, in cursory form, the most relevant history regarding the development of international law in the modern era.

A. The Westphalian International Legal System

The present international legal system had its genesis nearly 400 years ago. The 1648 Treaty of Westphalia, entered into by European state powers, marked the beginning of the "modern" era of international law, with the nation/state as the dominant actor in the creation of international law.[3] Not only did the nation/state emerge as the dominant actor in the West-phalian international legal system, but it was the only component of the system subject to international law.[4] The individual, although a subject of the state, was not considered to be subject to the international legal system. Instead, that system regulated the relationship between states, much like the state regulated the relationship between individuals.[5]

Importantly, states were regarded as sovereign entities. Accordingly, the internal affairs of the state, including the treatment of its citizens, could not be interfered with by other states.[6] The international law that developed between the states, moreover, was enforced primarily by means of voluntary compliance.[7]

Two primary sources of international law developed within this system: customary international law and law created by an agreement (e.g., treaty) between states. Before the development of law-making treaties, which nearly overwhelm the international system today, international law was based primarily on the customary behavior of states.[8] Customary international law is generally recognized as binding by the world community.[9]

Treaty law developed mainly as a negative law, prohibiting specific actions by signatory states. It dealt "primarily with political matters: peace treaties, treaties of alliance and friendship, neutrality treaties, and treaties settling territorial claims."[10] Today, treaty law has the same binding force as customary international law.[11] In fact, many treaties are merely codification of custom. For a treaty to become binding upon a domestic legal system, however, it is generally recognized that there must be an act of transformation, that is, "a government action by the state incorporating the treaty norm into its domestic law."[12]

B. The United Nations International Legal System

For the most part, the international law framework described above survives intact today.[13] However, since the arrival of the United Nations, the "many organizations that became its specialized and related agencies, which together constitute the UN System,"[14] have engendered important evolutionary change.[15] Perhaps the most significant developments have been the expanding number of treaties and other international agreements[16] and the inclusion of those treaties of matters pertaining primarily to the status of the individual.[17] In fact, contemporary international law is fundamentally "concerned with the development of institutionalized human rights."[18] No longer is the relationship between states the primary (or only) consideration in the development and codification of international law; rather international law now increasingly deals with the relationship between international governmental organizations (IGOs) and the individual.[19]

As a result, and under the tutelage of the UN, the subject matter of contemporary international law has evolved significantly from the pure Westphalian model:

[I]t differs . . . by a new quality of standards: prohibition on wars of aggression; prohibition of colonialism; the imposition of state responsibility for aggression and for other international violations such as genocide, racial discrimination, apartheid, et cetera; the international imposition of individual criminal responsibility for the violation of international law, as in acts of terrorism; the recognition of principles of self-determination of nations and peoples; the recognition and respect for human rights; and the peaceful resolution of international disputes. All of these standards are the basis of contemporary international law.[20]

Indeed, under the UN System, international law is now concerned with nearly every important aspect of modern society. International law no longer addresses only political matters, but "legal, social cultural, economic, technical and administrative matters as well."[21]

Furthermore, rather than springing from fairly straightforward sources—such as customary and treaty law—modern international law arises from a complicated morass of custom, treaty, formal agreement, informal agreement, debate, discussion and conference declarations of "norms:"

> International law is manifested in a large variety of different types of instruments, such as treaties, non-binding agreements, and declarations and decisions of international organs. All of these have the characteristics of "black letter" law in that the provisions can easily be read, although their binding force is widely differentiated and certainly cannot be defined by constructing hierarchies. There are also manifestations of the collective, coordinated or merely parallel will of states that can be determined by studying their actions in the light of expressed or implied motives. Thus, in addition to the distinctions between black and increasingly gray letter law, there is the distinction between binding or "hard" law and various "softer" forms. The international legislative or norm-making process is similarly structured, and also confusing in that there is no simple legislature and no single source of administrative law. Instead, there are a multitude of norm-makers at every geographic level (i.e. global, regional, subregional, and so on), as well as inchoate processes that create and identify international customary and perhaps even general principles of law. Furthermore, the rather clear-cut relationship that exists at the domestic level between processes and products (e.g., a legislative body produces statutes) is by no means as simple internationally, where all sorts of processes can produce, as direct outputs or as indirect by-products, various types of hard and soft and written and unwritten law.[22]

The UN, in short, has significantly complicated the scope and processes of international law. The range and pervasiveness of the UN's influence, moreover, may be expanding.

The end of the Cold War has brought significant changes to the UN system.[23] The United Nations is more visible[24] and the Security Council and General Assembly are more active.[25] During the Cold War, the Security Council and General Assembly often played a relatively minor role in international politics because controversies regarding the power of these bodies were magnified by the bi-polarity of the two superpowers.[26] During this period, the UN System could only encourage states to follow the principles it had adopted. Since the Cold War's demise, however, the UN has been thrust to the center of global affairs.[27] UN organs now take actions that go beyond mere "exhortation and admonition" on economic and social issues.[28] In particular, the UN's role in resolving disputes and functioning as a peacekeeper has increased dramatically.[29]

II. The International Law Context of UN Conference Declarations

United Nations conferences and their declarations fit into the "soft"—that is, not automatically binding—category of international law.[30] Although signed by representatives of the attending countries, conference declarations are generally perceived as instruments of exhortation to the world community regarding specified problems.[31] But, while technically "non-binding," UN conferences have a unique and important role in defining issues and allocating responsibilities with respect to the topics addressed.[32]

As is typical of most international "soft" law, conference declarations primarily use non-obligatory language.[33] Certain actions "should" rather than "must" or "shall" be taken.[34] Despite such language, however, conference declarations are considered to have some binding effect.[35] One of the best examples is the 1975 Final Act of the Helsinki Conference on Cooperation and Security in Europe, which specifically stated that it was not binding.[36] Nevertheless, the Act is often cited as the source of enforceable international legal obligations.[37]

In addition to using non-obligatory language, Conference declarations generally do not employ the enforcement mechanisms that have the greatest impact on the domestic policy of participating states. These mechanisms include reporting and supervision procedures,[38] facilitative mechanisms (such as armed peacekeeping forces),[39] expelling the state from the UN (or preventing it from taking part in its activities),[40] non-military enforcement (such as sanctions),[41] military enforcement,[42] and international judicial enforcement.[43] However, "a widely unappreciated fact [is that] a great deal of international law exists and is generally observed—usually without enforcement mechanisms."[44]

The subject matter of UN conferences involves issues of significant import that are generally being addressed contemporaneously by many other organizations and governments throughout the world. As such, the goals and recommendations articulated in a UN conference declaration may already be in an early (or advanced) stage of implementation by some states. Other states, not as far along in the goal formulation and implementation process, may use conference declarations as a planning and/or implementation outline. As a result, conference declarations almost certainly have a significant impact on the evolving discussions and planning decisions of world actors, although it is difficult to accurately assess the past or future effect of UN conferences on domestic law and policy.[45]

III. The Probable Impact of UN Conference Declarations on Domestic Policy

With the historical background of the international legal system and the context of UN declarations in mind, this article will now focus on four major areas where UN conference declarations have had and/or potentially may have a significant effect on domestic law and policy: first, by articulating perceived principles of customary international law; second, by directing the actions of UN agencies; third, by shaping the decisions and plans of domestic actors; and finally, by molding political and public opinion.

A. The Normative Influence of Conference Declarations

Customary international law, as noted, is considered binding upon states. As a result, a technically non-binding international instrument can become binding customary international law to the extent that it either crystallizes emergent rules of law or attracts uniform practice by participating states.[46]

Conference declarations are sometimes viewed as binding because they restate customary law. This concept is well illustrated by Principle 21 of the Stockholm Declaration, which was the product of the UN Conference on the Human Environment held in Stockholm, Sweden in 1972. The Declaration was regarded as nothing more than an advisory statement of purpose,[47] much like the exhortations of more recent UN conferences. Principle 21 of the Declaration, however, has "acquired the force of a substantive rule of customary international law."[48] Principle 21 provides:

States have, in accordance with the Charter of the United Nations and the principles of international law, the sovereign right to exploit their own resources pursuant to their own environmental policies, and the responsibility to ensure that activities within their jurisdiction or control do not cause damage to the environment of other States or of areas beyond the limits of national jurisdiction.

This Stockholm principle has been incorporated into "innumerable" international agreements and has been the basis for the expansion of international restrictions on transboundary pollution.[49]

Conference declarations, furthermore, can become binding even if they are not immediately perceived as restatements of customary law. "Customs," of course, are developed through uniformity of consistent practice revealed by one state's claims against another.[50] Accordingly, conference declarations may shape and direct the actions of nations, thereby facilitating the development of customary law. In the contemporary UN system, moreover, conference declarations may themselves be seen as evidence of uniform practice.[51] Some have even argued that the negotiation and drafting of an international instrument *creates* customary international law.[52]

Although in the past it took a rather long time for customary international law to develop, the acceleration of international interaction, brought on in part by the activities of the UN and other international governmental organizations, has resulted in the rather rapid creation of customary international law.[53] An extreme example of the rapidity with which customary international law may now be created is the emergence of the doctrine of "instant" customary international law.[54] Although disputed as a legitimate doctrine, it has been argued that a change to (or elimination of) an existing concept accepted as customary international law in a more recent nonbinding international instrument is an agreement that the older concept is no longer accepted by the international community.[55] As a result, the old concept is either no longer enforceable as customary international law or is changed "instantly" to be consistent with the new expression in the non-binding instrument.

Returning to Stockholm Principle 21, an example of "instant" customary law is illustrated in recent efforts to change that Principle at the Rio Conference.[56] The Rio Conference built upon many of the principles of the Stockholm Declaration. Principle 2 of the Rio Declaration on Environment and Development, for example, added "and developmental" to Stockholm Principle 21, so that states were authorized "to exploit their own resources, pursuant to their environmental *and developmental* policies."[57] Because Stockholm Principle 21, without the developmental component, is regarded as customary international law, the change made by Rio Principle 2 has been argued to be an "instant" change of customary international law that is binding on states—even though the Rio Declaration purportedly is not binding.[58] But, regardless of whether customary international law can be changed instantly by a non-binding international instrument, the debate reflects the reality that customary international law can be dramatically influenced by a non-binding instrument—without the passage of much time.

In addition to being a basis for the development of customary international law, conference declarations may establish "good practice standards" that are later codified into binding conventions or treaties.[59] There are numerous examples of declarations being converted later into binding instruments. The 1948 Universal Declaration of Human Rights was the foundation for the 1966 International Covenants on Economic, Social and Cultural Right and on Civil and Political Matters.[60] These covenants have been very influential. The 1963 Declaration of Legal Principles Governing the Activities of States in the Exploration and Use of Outer Space was the precursor to the 1967 Treaty on Principles Governing the Activities of States in the Exploration and Use of Outer Space.[61] Other types of non-binding international instruments, such as model codes and guidelines, also have been precursors to international treaties and laws enacted by states.[62]

B. The Impact Of Conference Declarations On UN Agency Action

The United Nations system operates with the assistance of many agencies that have been assigned a particular responsibility, such as implementing a treaty, convention, declaration or merely a provision of such a document. These agencies include, though are not limited to, the World Bank, International Monetary Fund (IMF), International Labor Organization (ILO), World Health Organization (WHO), UNICEF, and Habitat. Although some of these agencies enjoy at least some independence from the UN, such as the World Bank and IMF, they have their origins in the UN and continue to be tied, even if in only a limited sense, to its processes. These agencies, furthermore, have had an increasing impact on the domestic policy of purportedly sovereign states.

Much like agencies of domestic governments, UN agencies implement their mandates by directly applying an international instrument (e.g., a treaty or conference declaration), by promulgating and implementing its own regulations, or by implementing other internal UN regulations.[63] In recent years the development of agency regulations has dramatically increased.[64] In fact, regulations are now developed and implemented in areas that traditionally have been reserved to the control of states.[65]

UN agencies, moreover, use non-binding international instruments to expand the scope of their regulatory power.[66] By expanding the scope of international regulation through the use of non-binding international instruments, UN agencies—as a practical matter—have significantly relaxed the principle that no state can be bound to such documents without its consent.[67] As a result of this practice, "texts that are only recommendatory have as much effect as formal rules in channeling state conduct."[68]

UN agency regulations, furthermore, in certain instances, can lead to "a well-accepted body of international guidelines" articulating states' duties in a particular area—such as the environment.[69] These guidelines, articulated by a UN agency, can become internalized in the practices and legal systems of states.[70] The development of such guidelines can be initiated by a non-binding international instrument.[71]

In carrying out their expanding regulatory roles, UN agencies significantly impact the domestic policy of nations. Indeed, UN agencies may directly shape the relationship between the UN, domestic governments and private persons.[72] Those relationships are increasingly important as the world becomes more interdependent. At one extreme, a poor relationship between the UN or its agencies and domestic government can lead to a state being cut off from the benefits of participation in the international community or the denial of aid or other assistance. On the other extreme, a good relationship can lead to financial, technical and even military assistance.

UN agencies also use innovative techniques to reinforce the scope and influence of their actions. UN agencies coordinate their activities with other international governmental organizations, non-governmental organizations, and states sympathetic to their positions to draw upon the increased strength of combined efforts and resources. For example, a smaller UN agency, such as Habitat, might work with the much more powerful World Bank to achieve its goals. Through such coordination, financial and technical assistance can be made conditional on state compliance with a certain agency objective.[73] This has been called a "facilitative" process, by which the UN can induce state compliance on a matter to which the state may or may not have consented.[74]

This facilitative process has been described as follows in the population control context:

> [E]xperts working for donor organizations such as USAID, UNFPA, or the World Bank form alliances with like-minded local government officials, in-country researchers, or leaders of key [non-governmental organizations] such as family planning associations to propose policy solutions to recipient governments. A donor agency may appoint a population advisor to work with the government planners to formulate and implement an "official" demographic policy, with emphasis on the need to reduce birth rates through the promotion of family planning programs.[75]

This "facilitative" process can have not only a significant—but a debatable—impact. For example, Dr. Margaret Ogola, a physician and general practitioner in Kenya, feels that the efforts of UN bodies and other non-governmental organizations in providing condoms and I.U.D.s to curb population growth in Kenya is not only misdirected, but is causing the spread of AIDs:[76]

> [T]o quote one patient of mine, who was thoroughly horrified at the way Kenyans by the thousands are falling to AIDs, declared, "Doc, we are dying like flies!" The only answer that the non-governmental organizations (NGOs) and UN bodies have is to make condoms freely available, thus adding fuel to the flame.[77]

Regardless of how one feels about population control and the methods of UN agencies and NGOs in Kenya, Dr. Ogola's comments show that coordinated activities have significant effects.

UN conferences, finally, have played an important role in influencing the types of activities UN agencies pursue. The conferences have served as "catalytic agents in the process of redirecting and reforming the system."[78] Agency actions which deal in the subject area of a conference are strongly influenced by the conference and its declarations. This is well illustrated by the recent evolution of the international law of development.

The Vienna Conference Program of Action directs the World Bank to assess the social impacts, including human rights effects, of its financed projects.[79] In the past, the World Bank and the International Monetary Fund have been reluctant to consider human rights or other non-economic considerations in loan determinations.[80] However, in light of the controversy surrounding their continued connections with South Africa at the same time that the General Assembly was renouncing South Africa's policies of racial discrimination,[81] both the World Bank and the International Monetary Fund reconsidered that position. As a result of the South Africa controversy, the admonition by the Vienna conference, and other political pressures, the World Bank and other international development agencies now incorporate human rights into their guidelines.[82] Accordingly, UN conferences, along with other influences, enable states, international development agencies and non-governmental organizations to "interact and develop common standards to be imposed on national and international agencies engaged in the business of development."[83]

C. The Direct Effects of Conference Declarations on Domestic Policy

The two previous subsections of this Article dealt primarily with how UN conferences and their declarations may impact the *international* legal system, with subsequent consequences for domestic law and policy. This subsection, however, deals specifically with direct *domestic* enforcement and implementation of conference declarations. Without doubt, a conference declaration would have its greatest impact if it were enforceable through domestic courts.[84] It is generally recognized, however, that conference declarations have no direct binding force upon a domestic legal system. But that does not mean that conference declarations have little effect on domestic policy.

It has been argued that conference declarations should be enforced directly by domestic courts as "authoritative" interpretations of international law authorized by Articles 55 and 56 of the UN Charter.[85] If a state has ratified the UN Charter, as nearly all have, some argue that a declaration—under the obligatory force of the Charter—is binding upon the state. This theory, however, has enjoyed limited (or no) success to date. In the United States, for example, courts have routinely rejected it.[86] The non-obligatory language of conference documents suggests that the documents were never intended to create binding obligations and are merely recommendations for future action.

But, even if not formally binding, domestic courts *may* use conference declarations to "shape" domestic law. In the area of human rights,[87] advocates have argued that domestic courts can rely upon non-binding principles articulated in international instruments and conference declarations in construing domestic law, even if direct application of a particular principle is impossible.[88] In the United States, for example, where many of the most recent human rights treaties and conventions have no binding effect because they have not been ratified by the United States Senate, litigants have nevertheless invoked nonbinding UN documents. The approach, furthermore, has had some success.

In *Thompson v. Oklahoma*, the United States Supreme Court found that the execution of a 16-year-old for a brutal murder he committed at age 15 was "cruel and unusual punishment" prohibited by the Eighth Amendment to the United States Constitution. In finding the execution would violate the Eighth Amendment, the Court relied, in part, on the International Covenant on Civil and Political Rights and the American Convention on Human Rights—even though these documents are not binding in the United States because they have not been ratified.

The direct enforceability of formally non-binding instruments in domestic courts may be limited to gross violations of human rights.[89] It is important to note, however, that less than 60 years ago even gross violations of human rights were not considered challengeable on the basis of non-binding international declarations. It is, therefore, possible that—within the next 60 years—the principles articulated in the Istanbul, Beijing and Cairo conferences will carry the same weight and be used in a similar manner as the non-binding instruments in *Thompson*.[90]

Outside of the courts, conference declarations have had a significant impact on domestic governmental systems through implementation of the documents by the executive arms of domestic governments. Even though conference declarations are not binding, some governments have voluntarily implemented the articulated principles.[91] In fact, precisely because conference declarations are non-obligatory and therefore do not require formal domestic ratification like a treaty, the executive branch of a domestic government may be able to implement the declarations solely through executive action.[92] In the United States, for example, the Clinton Administration has formed an inter-agency task force and commission to implement the Beijing document. The task force and commission educate various federal agencies regarding Beijing recommendations and implement the document through domestic regulations. As a result, portions of the Beijing document have been incorporated directly into United States policy—without formal adoption of that document (or its stated objectives) by the United States legislature.[93]

D. The Effect of Conference Declarations on Political Discussion

Conference declarations have a significant impact beyond their role in developing customary law, directing the actions of UN agencies, and shaping domestic policy. Conferences and conference declarations influence public opinion, attract media attention, and generate political pressures that are important factors at all levels of the international and domestic legal systems.[94]

These are amorphous and interdependent factors.[95] Public opinion is strongly influenced by the amount of attention a conference is given by the media.[96] One concern with the Habitat II Conference in Istanbul, for example, is that—at least in the United States—it has received very little media attention. The Beijing Conference, by contrast, received vast media coverage. As discussed earlier, the Clinton Administration in the United States is now implementing the Beijing declaration. It would be difficult to determine what effect the media attention in Beijing has had on the Administration's current efforts.

However, political reality would dictate that the President of the United States would not implement the non-binding Beijing declaration without public support. Accordingly, the substantial media coverage of the Beijing Conference has undoubtedly had a role in defining women's issues for the American public.

Conferences not only influence the opinion of the general public, but the opinion and efforts of smaller groups and non-governmental organizations as well.[97] Declarations give individuals and groups who feel wronged by their government a tool to use in negotiations with the government. These groups, with the legitimizing support of a conference declaration, can be a strong force in swaying public opinion and governmental policies toward compliance with the declaration. Indeed, such groups—to the extent they gain popular support—can make it politically impossible for a government *not* to comply with principles stated in a UN conference declaration.[98]

Political pressures and public opinion, however, can also *prevent* a government from implementing a conference declaration. For example, in the context of population control, local citizens supported by their local leaders have sometimes resisted state population policies which threaten their survival strategies.[99] This resistance can essentially stifle state efforts to comply with policies enunciated at international population control conferences.[100] Therefore, the distribution of political power within a country can greatly influence whether a conference declaration will (or can) be implemented.

IV. Conclusion

To date, the signature of a state representatative on a UN conference declaration has not been seen as a clear indication of that state's acceptance of the principles therein contained or of the state's commitment to future compliance. Indeed, non-binding commitments may be made only to reach consensus or to "appease popular or 'politically correct' sentiment."[101] In fact, one writer has noted that in a conversation with a Latin American lawyer-diplomat, he was told that treaties signed by the lawyer's country were negotiated by the Ministry of Foreign Affairs and, when approved, were locked in a cabinet and almost never seen again.[102] Such an approach to the negotiation and finalization of UN conference declarations is unwise.

Although the precise influence of UN conference declarations on particular topical areas is debatable,[103] there can be little question but that conference declarations *do have* an impact. Each conference builds upon language used and objectives sought in preceding conferences and—as a result—forms an important link in a chain that inevitably encircles the international community.[104] The conferences, moreover, have become unique vehicles for mobilizing governmental and nongovernmental entities regarding global causes.[105] They also have been the impetus for the growth of new international law, particularly in the fields of human rights, development and the environment.[106] Perhaps most importantly, however, conference documents—although not formally binding upon participating states—over time develop the force of customary international law and serve as important resources in the interpretation (and sometimes development) of the domestic policy of participating nations.

This final point suggests that all participating nations should take very seriously indeed the language they incorporate into a UN declaration. Language may be precatory or exhortive today. That same language, however, may well become binding tomorrow.

NOTES

1. Nafis Sadik, *Reflections on the International Conference on Population and Development and the Efficacy of UN Conferences*, 6 COLO. J. INT'L L & POL'Y 249, 252-53 (1995) ("More than any previous events of their kind, these conferences have fostered the mobilization and participation of civil society and the private sector in the affairs of the international community. . . . The process has nurtured the growth of democracy at the national level and democratized processes at the international level increasing their transparency and accountability.").

2. Oscar Schachter, *The UN Legal Order: An Overview* in 1 UNITED NATIONS LEGAL ORDER 1, 3 (Oscar Schachter and Christopher C. Joyner, eds. 1995).

3. Oscar Schachter, *The UN Legal Order: An Overview* in 1 UNITED NATIONS LEGAL ORDER at 11 (Oscar Schachter and Christopher C. Joyner, eds. 1995). States have been dominant actors in international systems throughout history, but the Treaty of Westphalia is recognized as the event that placed states in their dominant position in modern international law. *See* Oleg I. Tiunov, *Concepts and Features on International Law: its Relationship to Norms of the National Law of the States*, 38 ST. LOUIS U. L.J. 915, 916 (1994) (states were the actors in the earliest international law).

4. Schachter, *supra* note 3, at 5.

5. Tiunov, *supra* note 3, at 916.

6. *Id.* At 916, 919; Richard B. Bilder, *An Overview of International Human Rights Law*, in GUIDE TO INTERNATIONAL HUMAN RIGHTS PRACTICE 3, 4 (Hurst Hannum, ed. 1992, 2nd ed.).

7. Tiunov, *supra* note 3, at 916; *see also* Bilder, *supra* note 6, at 12.

8. Paul Szasz, *General Law-Making Processes*, in 1 UNITED NATIONS LEGAL ORDER 35, 41 (Oscar Schachter and Christopher C. Joyner, eds. 1995); *see also* Tiunov, *supra* note 3, at 916-17 (Middle Ages international law was based on customs, religion and power. "International custom is the other great source of classical international law. Well before the development of law-making treaties, international law was based mostly on the customary behavior of states. . . .").

9. In the United States, customary international law is regarded to be a form of federal common law. It has the same status as treaty law, and has been held to be a component of the "law of the land" to which the Supremacy Clause of the United States Constitution requires adherence. *E.g.* Marc-Olivier Herman, *Fighting Homelessness: Can International Human Rights Law Make a Difference?*, 2 GEO. J. FIGHTING POVERTY 59, 72 (1994).

10. Martin A. Rogoff & Barbara E. Gauditz, *The Provisional Application of International Agreements*, 39 ME L. REV. 29 (1987).

11. Tiunov, *supra* note 3, at 916-17 (treaties are nearly as old as customary law and were entered into even at the earliest times and became quite prevalent in the middle ages.).

12. For role of treaties and other binding international instruments in domestic law see John H. Jackson, *Status of Treaties in Domestic Legal Systems: a Policy Analysis*, 86 AM. J. INT'L L. 310, 331 (1992). In the United States, a treaty must be ratified before it becomes binding. Ratification involves approval by the Senate and the signature of the President. Once a treaty is ratified in the US, it is treated the same as other federal law. Marc-Olivier, *supra* note 9, at 72. There are other states that require more than ratification, such as a further effort by the government to incorporate the treaty into domestic laws. See Tiunov, *supra* note 3, at 315 & n. 20.

13. Schachter, *supra* note 3, at 28 ("States are regarded as the principle actors in creating and applying law. Their independence and formal equality are taken as axiomatic. The principles of territorial integrity and *pacta sunt servanda*, as well as the customary rules of diplomatic intercourse, are accepted in the UN system, as they are in general international law. Also accepted is the basic divide between the international and domestic domains, though . . . the line between them may change or blur in particular cases.").

14. Szasz, *supra* note 8, at 40.

15. Tiunov, *supra* note 3, at 920, 922 (League of Nations was commencement of modern era but really was only a laboratory for the later real event: the creation of the UN). See also Bilder, *supra* note 6, at 4 (UN human rights focus causes dramatic increase in human rights documents). *See also id.* at 3 ("It is a new world in that only a century ago there were relatively few international organisations and any conception of a system or network was at best embryonic."). Hurst Hannum, *Human Rights*, in 1 UNITED NATIONS LEGAL ORDER 319 (Oscar Schachter and Christopher C. Joyner, eds. 1995); Tiunov, *supra* note 3, at 922-23; Schachter, *supra* note 3, at 23-24 ("[I]n today's perspective, it is not surprising that international legal regimes have proliferated in response to new needs and pressures. We are acutely aware of the impact of change through new technology, the population explosion . . . the emergence of new actors, the claims of former submerged peoples. . . . Matters once solely of local concern now have impact across national borders . . . [many problems] are perceived to require norms and procedures for resolving conflicts and collective action to render them effective. The availability of international institutions and the permanent conference machinery makes it virtually certain that law (hard or soft) will be created, adapted and applied to many of these problems.").

16. Rogoff & Gauditz, *supra* note 10, at 36-37 ("[A]ll types of international law, especially treaty law, are being created at an ever-increasing rate—indeed at a rate that sometimes seems to exceed the capacity of the international community (and especially its newer and less well-equipped members) to absorb and digest all the new norms.").

17. Schachter, *supra* note 3, at 24.

18. Tiunov, *supra* note 3, at 919.

19. *Id.*

20. *Id.*

21. Rogoff & Gauditz, *supra* note 10, at 29-30.

22. Szasz, *supra* note 8, at 35-36.

23. Schachter, *supra* note 3, at 1 ("There was good reason to take a close look as the ways in which international organizations produced and applied law in the many different fields of international concern [after the end of the Cold War].").

24. *Id.* ("The end of the Cold War gave new visibility to the United Nations and raised hopes for a more effective international legal order.").

25. *Id.* at 9, 12. ("The end of the Cold War brought to an end some of the old controversies [particularly regarding the power of the Security Council and General Assembly with respect to domestic matters and obligations of states on issues of self-determination and human rights] but new debates have arisen as a consequence of a more active Security Council and marked increase in cases involving UN sanctions and internal conflicts.").

26. Anthony Clark Arend, *The United Nations and the New World Order*, 81 GEO. L. J. 491, 492 (1993).

27. *Id.*

28. Schachter, *supra* note 3, at 15-16; *see also* Oscar Schachter, *United Nations Law*, 88 AM. J. INT'L L. 1, 10 (1994).

29. Of course, with this increased activity, the effectiveness of the UN is also being questioned more than in the past. This questioning arises from, among other things, the UN's failure or inability to resolve certain crises. *I.e.* Somalia and Bosnia. Questions regarding the UN's effectiveness may spill over into its activities in other areas—such as the role and place of UN conferences.

30. *See* Jiri Toman, *Quasi-Legal Standards and Guidelines for Protecting Human Rights*, in GUIDE TO INTERNATIONAL HUMAN RIGHTS PRACTICE 192 (Hurst Hannum, ed. 1992, 2nd ed.).

31. Conferences operate in much the same way the UN General Assembly operates, by attempting to reach a worldwide consensus through "inclusiveness in membership and mandate." Sadik, *supra* note 1, at 249 ("At the

---

local and national levels, the necessary consensus [for questions of rights, obligations and responsibilities] is achieved through numerous public and private political, economic, and social institutions and modalities. At the international level, however, there are few institutions suitable for implementing
such a consensus-building process. Because of its inclusiveness in membership and mandate, the United Nations General Assembly is the natural institution to which to turn. The General Assembly, aware of its inherent lim-
itations in this regard, has found it necessary to convene international
conferences for this purpose. United Nations (UN) conferences have a very
important role to play in meeting today's demands for global action: they
help define issues and allocate responsibilities, and the preparatory activities
for each conference serve to create the modicum of consensus necessary to
(at the very least) prevent even more global instability and disarray than exists today.").

32. *Id.*; James C.N. Paul, *The United Nations and the Creation of an International Law of Development*, 36 HARV. INT'L L.J. 307, 315 (1995); *see also*
Sadik, *supra* note 1, at 249.

33. Szasz, *supra* note 8, at 46.

34. *Id.* One of the primary reasons non-obligatory language is used is because a declaration is generally easier to formulate and consensus is more
easily reached without obligatory language. In addition, because declarations
do not have formal obligatory force, the procedures for producing them
often lack "the political safeguards that generally inform the international
legislative process." *Id.*

35. *Id.* at 38–39.

36. *Id.* at 46 n. 16.

37. *Id.*

38. Schachter, *supra* note 3, at 16.

39. *Id.* at 17.

40. *Id.*

41. *Id.* at 18.

42. *Id.* at 19.

43. *Id.*

44. Szasz, *supra* note 8, at 36.

45. David A. Wirth, *The Rio Declaration on Environment and Development:
Two Steps Forward and One Back, or Vice Versa?*, 29 GA. L. REV. 599, 649
(1995). ("If the history of the Stockholm Declaration teaches anything, it is
[that] the long-term significance of a nonbinding, aspirational statement of
purpose such as the Rio Declaration, the content of which may be responsive to immediate political and policy imperatives, cannot be predicted with

certainty. Moreover, the trajectory of discrete components of such an instrument may vary considerably as states make selective use of individual principles . . . States' experience in applying these principles may further elaborate, entrench, and codify these exhortations from both the policy and legal points of view.").

46. Schachter, *supra* note 3, at 4; Toman, *supra* note 30, at 192.

47. Wirth, *supra* note 45, at 602 & n. 10.

48. *Id.* at 620 & n. 56.

49. *Id.* at 600-601 ("The United Nations Conference on the Human Environment (Stockholm Conference), held in Stockholm from June 5 to 16, 1972, generally is considered a major turning point that 'marked the culmination of efforts to place the protection of the biosphere on the official agenda of international policy and law' ") (quoting Lynton K. Caldwell, International Environmental Policy: Emergence and Dimensions 55 (2nd ed. 1990).

50. Herman, *supra* note 9, at 72; Bilder, *supra* note 6, at 10 ("Customary international law is defined as a consistent practice in which states engage out of a sense of legal obligation.")

51. Schachter, *supra* note 3, at 4.

52. *Id.* Conference documents are viewed as significant international instruments because they are the result of consensus, following much debate and deliberation. Hannum, *supra* note 15, at 336 n. 77; see also Paul, *supra* note 32, at 315 ("Because world conferences provide potential opportunities for global popular participation, expert consultations, and, sometimes, vigorous debate, they can in theory, become unique vehicles to elaborate norms (cast in the form of legal instruments) governing development.") As such, conference declarations are imbued with a strong expectation that members of the international community will abide by them. As this expectation is justified by state practice, including activities within the UN organization, the principles of the document may—by custom—become binding upon a state.

53. Szaz, *supra* note 8, at 42.

54. *Id.*

55. *Id.*

56. Wirth, *supra* note 45, at 623 & nn.53-65.

57. *See Id.* at 620. The original text of Principle 21 is set out in the discussion preceding note 49.

58. It is generally accepted that the Rio Conference did change many well-accepted principles of customary international environmental law. *Id.* at 648.

59. Szasz, *supra* note 8, at 47, 98; Wirth, *supra* note 45, at 602-603.

60. Szasz, *supra* note 8, at 47 & n. 18.

61. *Id.*

62. *Id.*; Paul, *supra* note 32, at 317.

63. Hannum, *supra* note 15, at 339-40; Schachter, *supra* note 28, at 6.

64. *See* Szasz, *supra* note 8, at 36-37, 48; *see also* Section I historical section.

65. *Id.*

66. Schachter, *supra* note 3, at 7.

67. *Id.*

68. *Id.*; *see also* Frederic L. Kirgis, Jr. *Specialized Law-Making Processes*, in 1 UNITED NATIONS LEGAL ORDER 109 (Oscar Schachter and Christopher C. Joyner, eds. 1995) (UN organizations "have the capacity to channel the conduct of members in a way that are designed to advance, or at least not impede, an organization's attempts to achieve its states goals. [Norms] are promulgated or established by bodies recognized legitimate by the members, and as a result they command the respect, even if not always the strict obedience, of decision makers in national governments"). Some might argue that, by cooperating with UN agency regulations, a state is in fact consenting to the application of formal rules. Paul, *supra* note 32, at 311. To the extent states participate in the implementation of these regulations, states could be considered co-creators of the international regulation and consenting, through their conduct or acquiescence, to the agency action. Szasz, *supra* note 8, at 67; *see also* Paul, *supra* note 32, at 310-311. The effectiveness of the regulations, in fact, depends entirely on the "readiness of the member states to work together." Paul, *supra* note 32, at 311. A response to this view, however, would be that it ignores the "forces that have been mobilized within the UN system to influence both the content of the {international law of development] and efforts to enforce it." *Id.* at 310.

69. Wirth, *supra* note 45, at 637.

70. Szasz, *supra* note 8, at 48.

71. Wirth, *supra* note 45, at 637.

72. Schachter, *supra* note 28, at 6; *see also* Szasz, *supra* note 8, at 100.

73. Schachter, *supra* note 28, at 11.

74. *Id.*

75. RUTH DIXON-MUELLER, POPULATION POLICY & WOMEN'S RIGHTS 196 (1993).

76. Margaret Ogola, *Kenya: A Targeted Nation*, SOCIAL JUSTICE REVIEW, July /August 1994, 123, 124.

77. *Id.*

78. Sadik, *supra* note 1, at 253.

79. Paul, *supra* note 32, at 315 (citing United Nations, World Confer-

ence on Human Rights: Vienna Declaration and Programme of Action, Vienna, 14-25 June 1993, U.N. Doc. A/Conf. 157/24 (part 1 (1993) reprinted in 32 L.L.M. 1661. Art II(1)).

80. Klaus T. Samson, *Human Rights Co-ordination Within the UN System*, in THE UNITED NATIONS AND HUMAN RIGHTS 620, 663 (Philip Alston, ed. 1992).

81. *Id.*

82. *Id.* at 664; Paul, *supra* note 32, at 315-328.

83. Paul, *supra* note 32, at 309-310, 327 (citing S. Leckie, Towards an International Convention on Housing Rights: Options at Habitat II (American Society of International Law Papers on World Conference NO. 4, 1994)).

84. As mentioned earlier, international enforcement mechanisms as yet do not compare with the force of legitimacy of domestic ones. Schachter, *supra* note 28, at 14.

85. See Szasz, *supra* note 8, at 4; Herman, *supra* note 9, at 70-71; Jackson, *supra* note 12 at 331.

86. *See Sei Fuji v. California*, 242 P.2d 617 (Cal. 1952); *see also* Herman, *supra* note 9, at 71 & n. 157.

87. Bilder, *supra* note 6, at 6-7 ("[T]here are a great number of international declarations, resolutions, and recommendations relevant to international human rights that have been adopted by the United Nations or by other international organizations or conferences. While these instruments are not directly binding in a legal sense, they establish broadly recognized standards and are frequently invoked in connection with human rights issues.").

88. Herman, *supra* note 9, at 72.

89. *Id.*

90. Herman, *supra* note 9, at 72-73 ("Perhaps the most realistic and effective litigation strategy is to suggest to a court that the norms of international human rights law are guides to interpreting federal, state, and local laws.") See also Bilder, *supra* note 6, at 11 ("[N]ational courts may be responsive to arguments that domestic law should be interpreted consistently with international human rights standards, particularly in cases where an inconsistent interpretation, even if not technically a breach of law, might nevertheless be politically embarrassing.") See also Jackson, *supra* note 12, at 312 & n. 12.

91. Jackson, *supra* note 12, at 313.

92. *See* Rogoff & Gauditz, *supra* note 10, at 33; Toman, *supra* note 30, at 193.

93. *See* Szasz, *supra* note 8, at 98.

94. *See* Schachter, *supra* note 28, at 22–23; Toman, *supra* note 30, at 208 (the effectiveness of international standard setting instruments "varies in direct proportion to the extent they are publicized, utilized, and taken seriously by those affected by them.").

95. *See* Schachter, *supra* note 28, at 22.

96. *Compare* Hannum, *supra* note 15, at 23.

97. *See* Schachter, *supra* note 28, at 22; Hannum, *supra* note 15, at 338; Dixon-Mueller, *supra* note 75, at 197.

98. *See* Bilder, *supra* note 6, at 11.

99. *See* Dixon-Mueller, *supra* note 75, at 197.

100. *Id.*

101. Neil H. Afran, *International Human Rights Law in the Twenty First Century: Effective Municipal Implementation or Paen to Platitudes,* 18 FORDHAM INT'L L.J. *1756, 1758 (1995).*

102. Jackson, *supra* note 12, at 322 n. 70.

103. *See* Schachter, *supra* note 28, at 161 ("While the results of these [human rights] efforts remain uncertain (and to some, questionable), they do evidence the importance attributed to the human rights movement and idealogy."); Szasz, *supra* note 8, at 107 ("Partly because the record keeping of the international legislative process remains woefully fragmented and underdeveloped, it is difficult to establish anything like a complete catalog of all its accomplishments, or even to determine in which fields it has been most productive and effective.").

104. *See* Sadik, *supra* note 1, at 252.

105. *Id.; see also* Paul, *supra* note 32 at 315.

106. *See* Paul, *supra* note 32 at 327.

Remarks in Hearings of Committee II of the Second United Nations Conference on Human Settlements (Habitat II)

Richard G. Wilkins

Instanbul, Turkey, 10 June 1996

Mr. Chairman, Honorable Delegates, as a Professor of Law at Brigham Young Universtiy and Representative of the Caucus For Stable Communities, it is an honor to address International Law and the Family.

International law deals with the vital issues that arise as women, men and children live together in national and international communities. The traditional family is the necessary foundation for these larger communities because it is the sanctuary where women and men learn cooperation, sacrifice, love, and mutual support; it is the training ground where children learn the public virtues of responsibility, work, fair play and social interdependence.

International law and the family, therefore, are inextricably linked. Disregarding this link places both the law and families in peril. Dialogues between family-based non-governmental organizations and governmental organs, however, can reduce this risk. That cooperation, furthermore, is essential as the regulatory role of UN Conferences expands.

For example, the Habitat Agenda could reshape the contours of international law. Such Conference Documents can be seen as restatements of binding customary international law.

Conference Documents can also significantly alter local law, both through voluntary compliance and by directing the development of domestic law. These documents, finally, address topics—such as housing—that previously were left to local decisionmakers.

This expansion in the role of Conference Documents raises serious questions related, not only to their substantive content, but to the democratic process by which the documents are crafted. As a lawyer and a family advocate, these issues are troubling.

There is substantial distance between those drafting and implementing a Conference Document and those enjoying the benefits or bearing the burdens of that drafting and implementation. In a local arena, affected families have relatively easy access to the decisionmakers who can provide redress. Not so on the international front, where many are readily confused by complex international procedure. Unless this gap between international government and the family is closed, international government is in danger of losing touch with—and perhaps doing substantial harm to—its citizens.

Non-governmental organizations (NGOs) may help fill this gap. The many views put forward by NGOs and their associated caucuses reduce the risk of regulatory error, to the substantial benefit of both international law and citizens living under that law. For this process to work, however, all voices must be heard. There is, moreover, one important voice that—at least in my professional legal opinion—has not been given adequate attention in the international lawmaking process: the voice of the traditional family.

There is a fundamental connection between the effectiveness of the international—indeed, any—legal system and the reinforcement of strong, stable families. This Conference has spent substantial time debating the infrastructure essential for sustainable communities. Similar close attention must be paid to what I would call "intra-structure." This "intra-structure" is built from the fundamental values fostered by strong families.

Family-centered advocacy groups can work positively with government to facilitate sustainable communities. One of the more controversial issues in the debate over the Habitat Agenda is the question of teenage reproductive health education and services. Unplanned teenage pregnancies obviously burden community sustainability. While some pragmatically turn to contraception and abortion, there are family-centered government initiatives that not only address this serious problem but recognize the sanctity of life.

As one example, family advocacy groups in the United States persuaded Congress to authorize a family-based sexual abstinence approach to teenage pregnancy prevention. The enabling legislation specifically recognized that, quote:

> . . . the family is the basic social unit in which the values and attitudes of adolescents concerning sexuality and pregnancy are formed. . . .

A program set up by Northwest Family Services included facilitating discussions between parents and children on human sexuality, the advantages of premarital abstinence and the medical facts of fetal development. A five-year statistical analysis of the program, conducted by Dr. Stan Weed of the Institute for Research and Evaluation, found significant improvements in parent-child communication and, even more importantly, a substantial decrease in teenage pregnancy.

Cooperation between family-oriented NGOs and those implementing Conference Documents can produce these kinds of positive results and also help avoid government interventions that destabilize families and ultimately the community itself.

For example, a well-intentioned international mandate to provide adequate housing for women and children, prompted by the deplorable conditions facing abandoned women and children, may—in a perverse twist—exacerbate rather than resolve the very problem it addresses. Such a program, unless drafted and administered with the needs, role and function of the family in mind, may encourage other men to abandon their wives and children to the State, thereby not only undermining the family but rendering the goal of a sustainable community increasingly difficult.

The issues before this Conference are complex. Their proper resolution will be greatly aided by careful attention to the views and perspectives of the non-governmental sector. In that process, I urge you not to forget the most basic and fundamental community of all: the family.

Arab Announcement on Family Concept and Form Introduced in UN Conference on Sustainable Development of Human Settlements

Instanbul, Turkey, 12 June 1996

The Heads and Members of Arab delegations participating in the UN Conference on Sustainable Development of Human Settlements in Istanbul 3 - 14 / 6 / 1996. Announce in regard to paragraphs 22 ter, 27A ter, 87A, 92 bis, 96D bis, 92 included in the conference document and similar paragraphs dealing with concept of family, form, health awareness and reproduction:

1. **Proceeding** of the Arab declaration of sustainable development of human settlements (Rabat Declaration). Also the Arab Coordination meeting for said conference in Tunis and Attachments of Reports and recommendations of advisory committees and working groups established by the Council of Arab Ministers of Housing and Reconstructions;

2. **Proceeding** from the fact that the Arab world, the cradle of the earliest human civilizations and the birthplace of divine religions. Moreover, it possesses deep-rooted cultural and civilisational capabilities and divinely-inspired legislations stipulating the preservation of human dignity as a sacred duty;

3. **Convinced** of the importance of preserving the religious, cultural and civilization heritage of the Arab

world in general, and its urban culture and heritage in specific;

4. **Convinced** of prominent principles of family forms and legal (generation) and cohesiveness provided by the Holy Islamic Sharyyat and abiding by the culture and understanding of the pillars of Islamic society;

5. **Explaining** the Arab views of family form and concept.

As introduced in the above-mentioned paragraphs in this declaration. The heads and members of the Arab delegation. Decide on their behalf the following:

1. **Enforcing** that human being, is the objective and maker of development, and therefore, must be the center of all interests pertaining to sustainable development. Every human being has the right to live, within human settlements, a healthy and productive life, that is, compatible with religious values which advocate justice, peace, love and mutual responsibility;

2. **Enforcing** that the family is the fundamental nucleus of the society. All appropriate conditions must be provided to maintain its safety, to upgrade its living standard, to safeguard its values and cohesiveness, and to provide it with adequate housing, job opportunities, and a dignified living of all its members, including the elderly and handicapped;

3. **The family** starts with a man and a woman bonded according to social and religious norms. The woman undertakes a very important role, not only as a mother but also as a prominent effective contributor in achieving sustainable development and empowered in all tasks in this regard;

4. **The children** have all basic rights in a healthy, happy, and safe life and must be provided proper housing, health care, education, family raising, and entertainment;

5. **The youth** are the fundamental elements in society; development and production must be provided with wide-ranging opportunities to exercise their right to education and training, and to secure work and adequate housing in order to start and maintain families. They must be enabled for effective and collective participation in all activities of sustainable development;

6. **The grown** fetus have the full right to live and be raised according to religious and local norms, proper and complete health care to them and their mothers must be provided. Food and adequate living and proper conditions for raising infants must be provided under the auspices of them their parents as much as possible.

Proceeding from the principles explained in this declaration advancing to achieve the goals of this conference.

—Sustainable development of human settlements in urbanizing a world moving towards progress.

—Adequate housing for all.

Proceeding from the above said understandings, the heads and members of Arab delegations announce:

1. **Working** to implement the decisions mentioned in this announcement.

2. **Working** to enforce the family concept and form of its religions traditional understanding and its requirements in providing social, health, education, entertainment and living and its requirement in providing proper housing and dignified life.

Statement at the Second United Nations Conference on Human Settlements (Habitat II)

by the Right Honourable John Gummer MP
Secretary of State for the Environment
United Kingdom

Instanbul, Turkey, 13 June 1996

Mr. President, Excellencies, Distinguished Delegates.

The theme of sustainable development, and its place in providing a secure future for our cities and towns rightly deserves to be a central concern of our time. Like the natural environment, settlements from the largest city to the smallest village represent invaluable assets. We hold them in trust for future generations. If we add to their quality the inheritance of generations to come will be the greater.

Yet it is people for whom cities are created. They are above all places for people. Even the most ramshackle and poverty-stricken are seen as beacons of hope by people. Hope of a better life, better education, better health. For many millions of individuals, those hopes are still dashed, and it is our purpose in this Conference to reverse that situation and to make these hopes a reality.

I start with people because too often we are preoccupied by process and institution, design and infrastructure. All these are vital, but only to the extent that they provide for the needs of people. At its best, urban living provides for human creativity and civilised living. At its worst, it is the negation of both. Men and women living cheek by jowl in the city share their lives and their dreams, their skills and their thoughts, in the creativity which only close human contact can ensure.

Yet in our huge conurbations, where poverty and deprivation, ignorance and disease, reign supreme, there is no room for anything else but survival and human beings are seen not as worthy in their own right, individuals with hopes and aspirations, but instead, as problems—statistics so large that solutions seem impossible.

That is why Habitat II is so important. It reminds us of the worth of every human being. It seeks therefore to make a reality of the city as a beacon of hope. It recognises that the demands for quality of design and architecture, of infrastructure and education, are not high-minded hopes but severely practical necessities if cities are to be proper places in which to live.

We have expressed this in the UN's terms of "rights". Such terms are not adequate. A proper appreciation of the worth of individuals insists not upon rights but upon obligations. For me, the right to decent housing is better stated as an obligation laid on all of us to forward those conditions which make decent housing possible.

A proper belief in the worth of every individual is the necessary precursor of the partnership which alone will regenerate our cities. A partnership between local government and national government, between business, industry and voluntary organisations, but above all, partnership with people. It is when even the poorest see that they have a part to play, that they can take ownership, that their contribution, however small, is a necessary part of the achievement of the new city. It is then that we have begun on the only process which can make the ideals of Habitat II a success.

When I presided over the award ceremony earlier on, the

common factor among all these uncommon projects was that they respected the ability of even the least privileged to contribute to their regeneration. Whether it is women's cooperative banking in India or sustainable communities in the Netherlands, they share the single vision of a world in which each individual is counted worthy enough to contribute.

This is the culture of life which, all over the UK, is rejuvenating our cities. Tenants choosing the kind of homes they want and managing them, shared ownership, self-build community action, partnership, multi-nationals sitting down with amenity groups, government acting on plans prepared by housing association tenants—this is the culture of life which respects individuals enough to expect them to do their bit. For, too often, elites—whether good-hearted philanthropists or ideologically-driven Marxists—have sought to better other people's lot in ways which they—the elites—think best. Habitat II is about empowering people and that starts by respecting people.

Sadly, however, the culture of death is still with us in those places where we still destroy communities to put people into housing which we think is good for them, instead of homes which foster communities and reflect individual hopes and aspirations, in those places where those who are inconvenient are ignored or oppressed, the street children who disappear, the old and the young who die when they could have lived, the babies whom we kill even before they have a chance to live.

Habitat II can point to a renewal of hope in the city, a rediscovery of that sense of excitement, opportunity, community, prosperity and culture which are found there—whether it is Milan or Manila, Birmingham or Buenos Aires, we have the same battle to build cities which respect people and their worth. That is why we have to battle against the claustrophobia of congestion and the dreariness of design, the emptiness of